Taste of Home
EVERYDAY
AIR FRYER

100+ RECIPES FOR WEEKNIGHT EASE

Taste of Home

EVERYDAY
AIR FRYER

100+ RECIPES FOR WEEKNIGHT EASE

TASTE OF HOME BOOKS • RDA ENTHUSIAST BRANDS, LLC • MILWAUKEE, WI

©2021 RDA Enthusiast Brands, LLC.
1610 N. 2nd St., Suite 102, Milwaukee WI 53212-3906
All rights reserved. Taste of Home is a registered
trademark of RDA Enthusiast Brands, LLC.

Visit us at **tasteofhome.com** for other
Taste of Home books and products.

International Standard Book Number:
978-1-61765-951-5

Library of Congress Control Number:
2020936338

Executive Editor: Mark Hagen
Senior Art Director: Raeann Thompson
Editor: Amy Glander
Designer: Jazmin Delgado
Copy Editor: Amy Rabideau Silvers

Cover Photo
Photographer: Dan Roberts
Set Stylist: Stacey Genaw
Food Stylist: Sarah Farmer

Pictured on front cover and title page:
Nashville Hot Chicken, p. 178; Crispy Potato Chips, p. 37
Pictured on back cover:
Taco Twists, p. 226; Raspberry French Toast Cups, p. 73;
Turkey Club Roulades, p. 169; Sweet Potato Fries, p. 96;
S'mores Crescent Rolls, p. 235; Bacon Cheeseburgers, p. 203

Printed in USA
7 9 10 8 6

CONTENTS

MORE WAYS TO CONNECT WITH US:

Our Test Kitchen tested recipes using six different air-fryer models.

We discovered cook times can vary dramatically across different brands.

To accommodate this variance, the recipes in this book have a wider than normal range of suggested cook times. Begin checking the food at the first time listed in the recipe and adjust as needed.

SAY GOODBYE TO YOUR DEEP FRYER, AND PREPARE THE CRISPIEST, CRUNCHIEST, TASTIEST "UNFRIED" FOODS EVER. LET THIS BOOK BE YOUR GUIDE.

Do you love kitchen gadgets? If the answer is yes, chances are you have an air fryer. These small but mighty countertop appliances have been around for about a decade, but they've recently picked up steam for their ability to "fry" foods with little to no oil.

If you're new to this method of "frying" food, fear not. Now you can cook with confidence with the 112 delicious air-fried recipes inside *Taste of Home Everyday Air Fryer*. With this brand-new cookbook in hand, it's never been easier to lighten some of your favorite comfort foods. That's because the air method practically eliminates the need for oil, leaving you with crispy chicken tenders, breaded fish fillets, toasted ravioli, onion rings, potato chips and other fun foods, all without the unpleasant mess or excess fat of deep-fat frying.

But this appliance isn't just for creating a healthier alternative

to cooking traditionally deep-fried foods. You can also make other tried-and-true favorites with this cool tool. Cook up a juicy air-fryer steak. Start your Saturday morning with a batch of sizzling bacon. Or satisfy your sweet tooth by air-frying chocolate chip cookies.

Air-fryer aficionados know this kitchen tool is good for more than making recipes from scratch. It's also awesome for reheating foods like french fries and other takeout faves. Put it to work cooking frozen foods—from mozzarella sticks to chicken wings—in a flash. The creative possibilities are endless!

HOW DOES IT WORK?

An air fryer is basically a mini countertop convection oven. The food goes into a basket (similar to the one you'd use in a deep fryer), but instead of hot oil, the food is blasted with hot air to create that crunchy texture everyone craves.

Because of its small size, air fryers heat up fast. An air fryer is ready to cook after about three minutes of heating.

The main unit holds a heating coil and a fan, and food is placed in the removable fryer basket below. Hot air rushes down and around the food in the basket. This rapid circulation makes the food crisp, as deep-frying does, with little or no added oil.

Some air fryers have digital screens with the setting options; others have simple time and temperature dials. Choose the style you are most comfortable using.

Some air fryers can perform additional functions besides air-frying. These models are often more expensive and larger in size. Choose the one that best suits your needs.

Many models are sized to cook for one or two people. Some have a larger capacity, allowing you to cook for up to four people at a time.

With a smaller appliance, you have to cook in batches, so be sure to account for that in your planning.

Read the instruction manual before getting started.

Remove all packing materials and tape from both outside and inside the appliance. Look up into the heating element (see photos on page 8) to make sure no stray material is lodged in the coil or fan. This can cause the appliance to smoke.

Thoroughly wipe down the heating coil before the first use to remove any residue.

(see photos on page 8)

COOK LIKE A PRO

- Verify the temperature, as it will vary among models, just as it does with ovens. Test your air fryer before using to see if it runs above or below the selected temperature setting.

- Allow plenty of room. Cook food in a single layer, with room for air to circulate. For crispy results, don't forget to flip, rotate or shake the basket's contents halfway through cooking.

- Use a thermometer when cooking meat. Air-fried meats brown nicely, so it may look done before reaching an appropriate temperature on the inside.

AIR-FRYER PARTS

A. Heating coil (also shown bottom right)
B. Fan (inside unit)
C. Basket
D. Maximum fill line
E. Temperature setting
F. Time setting
G. Power
H. Basket release

HOW TO CLEAN YOUR AIR FRYER

Basket: The basket, its holder and any dividing compartments that came with your air fryer are dishwasher safe. After each use, allow the air fryer to cool. Remove the cooled basket, tray and pan, and wash them as you would any other dish.

Exterior: When it comes to cleaning the outside of an air fryer, a simple soapy wipe-down will do. Unplug the appliance and gently wipe with a damp cloth. That's it!

Heating Coil: If there is oil or residue on the heating coil, let the unplugged machine cool, then wipe the coil with a damp cloth—just as you would with the heating element on an electric stove.

Unexpected Mess? If your cooking project was a bit messier than usual or the machine has developed an odd odor, your air fryer may require a deeper cleaning.

HERE'S WHAT THE BUTTONS ON YOUR AIR FRYER ACTUALLY MEAN

Thanks to the weeknight-changing magic of air fryers, you can serve up a meal in minutes. Plus, you can cook almost everything in this gadget—from cheesy breakfast egg rolls to a plate of Nashville hot chicken. It's basically a home cook's dream come true.

The best reason to jump on the air-fryer bandwagon is the intuitiveness of the most popular models. To help you become an air-fryer pro, we're breaking down the buttons and functions you'll find on most of the handy ovens. Use this helpful guide to master the air fryer's most common functions.

▶❙❙ Button

The "Cook / Pause" button is one you'll find on compact models like this. This important button allows you to pause cooking so you can turn food (say, chicken wings or fish fillets) to ensure everything is cooked all the way through. It also lets you shake the contents of the basket (fries, broccoli, Tater Tots, etc.) to achieve maximum crispiness. Use this button to check the temperature for doneness when cooking meat, poultry or fish.

-/+ Button

Look for single or dual -/+ buttons to adjust time and temperature. On many popular models, there is a button to shift from time or temperature to adjust both. On models without an LCD screen, the -/+ buttons are replaced by knobs or dials.

Keep Warm

Many home cooks use the air fryer like a second oven, cooking up a tasty appetizer or side dish to go along with the entree baking away in the actual oven. This "Keep Warm" function does exactly that for a set amount of time—usually 30 minutes.

Food Presets

You may own an air fryer with buttons for certain foods, including frozen french fries, chicken or fish. If you're an air-fryer newbie, they can certainly give you an idea of what to cook in your new machine! The presets give you the ability to cook whatever you want without second-guessing because the temperature and time are already set.

Before setting and forgetting, it's helpful to check out your machine's manual. Every preset is set for a specific

amount of food in grams, so for a double serving of chicken—or a smaller amount of frozen fries—you will need to adjust for time.

Roast or Broil

The option to roast vegetables or brown meat in an air fryer is becoming more common with larger air-fryer models. Use the Roast setting when you're ready to place a marinated piece of meat—let's say a beef chuck roast—into the air-fryer basket. In a conventional oven, you would typically brown the meat before baking. With an air fryer, you can skip that step. The constant flow of hot air creates a gorgeous, caramelized exterior on its own. Just remember to flip the meat and/or vegetables halfway through. Check the interior temps to know when it's ready to take out, too.

Dehydrate

Dehydrating typically can be done in an air fryer, with food placed on an air-fryer rack. With the Dehydrate option, you can create your own dried fruit or beef jerky right at home! This preset option cooks and dries food using a lower temperature for hours.

AIR-FRYER COOKING TIPS

New to air-frying? Here are a few secrets for success.

Check the temperature.

Just like with full-size ovens, temperatures may vary among air-fryer models. Test your air fryer to see if it runs above or below the selected temperature setting. You'll want the fryer nice and hot for those air-fried eggplant fries.

Know your air fryer's cooking times.

Since air-fryer temperatures vary, so do cook times. That's why our air-fryer recipes have wider time ranges. To find cooking times for your air fryer, you'll need to experiment. Start checking the food at the shortest time, and check back a little later if it's not done.

Give it a shake (or a flip).

To help food crisp, always turn, rotate or shake contents in the air-fryer basket (just like flipping french fries, fish fillets or chicken strips when cooking in a traditional oven).

Cook food in a single layer for best results.

Allow plenty of air circulation to get even cooking and crispy results. One exception where you can stack and pack foods is if you're roasting veggie side dishes in the air fryer. For instance, you can load the basket with a pound of Brussels sprouts and roast them at 350° for 12-15 minutes, stirring once.

Seeing smoke? Here's what to do.

Don't panic. Simply unplug the air fryer and remove the food basket. Make sure no food is lodged in the heating coil. Return food to the air fryer and continue cooking. If smoke persists, there may be oil or residue on the heating element. Unplug the machine, cool, and then wipe the coil clean with a damp cloth, just like the heating coil on an electric stove. In the future, make sure to clean your air fryer regularly.

Use a thermometer when cooking meat.

Food can brown nicely on the outside before reaching an appropriate temperature on the inside, so check the temp with a thermometer for food safety. The same goes for previously frozen foods and fresh ones, as well.

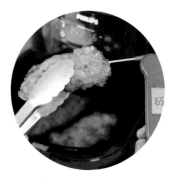

Bake up a little treat.

Yes, you can bake homemade cookies—and other treats—in the air fryer! All it takes is a few minutes and chilled dough on stand-by. Models differ in their "baking" functions, so test just one or two cookies first. You may need to adjust the temperature or cooking time.

Take advantage of it when cooking for one or two.

Air fryers are small, making them great when you're cooking a low-yield meal. Any more than that, and you may have to cook in batches.

11 COMMON AIR-FRYER MISTAKES

They promise low-fat cooking with extra-crispy results, but if you don't use your air fryer properly, results may be less than dazzling.

Too much stuff on the counter.
It might be small—and mighty—but air fryers need their space. That's because these mini ovens rely on a constant flow of air to move the high-temp heat around the food for all-over crispness. Make sure your air fryer has at least 5 inches of space on all sides. And keep it on a stable surface, so the vibration won't send it tumbling onto the floor.

Not preheating the air fryer.
Like an oven, an air fryer needs to be hot to properly cook the moment the door shuts. If it's too cold, the final food may suffer. Check your recipe's suggested temperature before getting started. Go ahead and turn the air fryer on, so it is plenty hot when you're ready to use it. It won't take long—that small space can reach the right temperature in under five minutes.

Using too much oil.
Most air fryers call for only a teaspoon or two of oil. If too much is added, you won't get the results you're looking for. Remember that an air fryer is not a deep fryer. But it achieves similar results by circulating very hot air around food as it bakes.

Not using any oil.
You can have too much oil—and you can have too little. Most recipes will recommend the amount that's right for that dish, but when in doubt, give your food a quick spritz. Oil is a great medium to transfer heat. Spritzing a little bit of nonstick oil spray will help the food get crisp and brown.

The foods are too wet.
Deep fryers can expel moisture from foods like batters, but an air fryer isn't capable of that. Don't put limp, wet veggies in an air fryer, as they will not crisp up properly. Instead, use your air fryer to quickly crisp already breaded or crunchy foods, such as breaded chicken tenders or Brussels sprouts.

The foods are too light.
An air fryer's moving air means lighter foods could float and fly around inside the appliance. You don't want something lightweight like spinach, as it starts to fry, to get caught in the heating coil and start to burn.

Too much food in the basket.
The machine needs air around it, and the food does, too. If you overcrowd the basket, the food won't have enough exposed surface area. Where the hot air meets the surface of the food

and any oil is where the cooking (and flavor) happens. Because air fryers cook quickly, you can cook in small batches—and that will ensure each piece has the best possible flavor and texture.

The food is too small.
Food that is too small could slip right through the slots in the air-fryer basket and fall onto a heating element. The pieces will burn quickly, which could fill your food—and your kitchen—with fumes and smoke. Keep all of your ingredients about the size of a Brussels sprout. When in doubt, drop the food in the basket and give it a shake over the sink. If anything slips out, don't put it in the air fryer.

Fatty foods drip.
You might have purchased an air fryer to complement a lower-fat eating plan, but you can also use it to fry up high-fat favorites like burgers, sausages and bacon. Before you hit the start button, make sure you put water in the bottom of the cavity under the frying basket. This way, when fat drips onto the hot surface, it will hit water—not hot metal—preventing fat from burning and creating a smoky mess.

Cooking in the air fryer without cleaning it.
A dirty air fryer can be dangerous for your stomach and your nose. There's a much higher risk of food contamination if you do not clean your air fryer between uses.

CHAPTER 1

SNACKS & APPETIZERS

Everyone loves the opportunity to sample different and delicious foods at parties and gatherings. With your air fryer, it's never been easier to serve up classic appetizers and finger foods with less fat and fewer calories than their oil-immersed counterparts. Check out these tasty recipes for chicken wings, roll-ups, meatballs and more.

BEEF TAQUITOS

I love these zesty appetizers. They're great for any occasion, whether it's taco night with the family or a Mexican-themed fiesta with friends. Spice them up by adding sliced jalapenos, if desired.

—Mark Webber, Valdez, AK

PREP: 20 MIN. • COOK: 15 MIN./BATCH • MAKES: 10 SERVINGS

2 large eggs
½ cup dry bread crumbs
3 Tbsp. taco seasoning
1 lb. lean ground beef (90% lean)
10 corn tortillas (6 in.), warmed
Cooking spray
Optional: Salsa and guacamole

1. Preheat air fryer to 350°. In a large bowl, combine eggs, bread crumbs and taco seasoning. Add beef; mix lightly but thoroughly.

2. Spoon ¼ cup beef mixture down the center of each tortilla. Roll up tightly and secure with toothpicks. In batches, arrange taquitos in a single layer on greased tray in air-fryer basket; spritz with cooking spray. Cook 6 minutes; turn and cook until meat is cooked through and taquitos are golden brown and crispy, 6-7 minutes longer. Discard toothpicks before serving. If desired, serve with salsa and guacamole.

1 taquito: 168 cal., 6g fat (2g sat. fat), 65mg chol., 336mg sod., 17g carb. (1g sugars, 2g fiber), 12g pro.

SWEET & SPICY MEATBALLS

I'm always on a quest for speedy meatballs that pack a sweet and savory punch.
These are a snap to pull together and can be served over rice or buttered noodles.
—*Tami Kuehl, Loup City, NE*

PREP: 30 MIN. • COOK: 15 MIN./BATCH
MAKES: 3 DOZEN MEATBALLS (ABOUT 1 CUP SAUCE)

⅔ cup quick-cooking oats
½ cup crushed Ritz crackers
2 large eggs, lightly beaten
1 can (5 oz.) evaporated milk
1 Tbsp. dried minced onion
1 tsp. salt
1 tsp. garlic powder
1 tsp. ground cumin
1 tsp. honey
½ tsp. pepper
2 lbs. lean ground
   beef (90% lean)

SAUCE
⅓ cup packed brown sugar
⅓ cup honey
⅓ cup orange marmalade
2 Tbsp. cornstarch
2 Tbsp. soy sauce
1 to 2 Tbsp. Louisiana-style
   hot sauce
1 Tbsp. Worcestershire sauce

1. Preheat air fryer to 380°. In a large bowl, combine the first 10 ingredients. Add beef; mix lightly but thoroughly. Shape into 1½-in. balls.

2. In batches, arrange meatballs in a single layer on greased tray in air-fryer basket. Cook until lightly browned and cooked through, 12-15 minutes. Meanwhile, in a small saucepan, combine sauce ingredients. Cook and stir over medium heat until thickened. Serve with meatballs.

1 meatball with 1½ tsp. sauce: 90 cal., 3g fat (1g sat. fat), 27mg chol., 170mg sod., 10g carb. (7g sugars, 0 fiber), 6g pro.

BREADED PICKLES

Are you a fan of deep-fried pickles? You'll love this version. Dill pickle slices are coated with panko bread crumbs and spices, then air-fried until crispy. Dip them in ranch dressing for an appetizer you won't soon forget.
—*Nick Iverson, Denver, CO*

PREP: 20 MIN. + STANDING • COOK: 15 MIN./BATCH • MAKES: 32 SLICES

32 dill pickle slices
½ cup all-purpose flour
½ tsp. salt
3 large eggs, lightly beaten
2 Tbsp. dill pickle juice
½ tsp. cayenne pepper
½ tsp. garlic powder
2 cups panko bread crumbs
2 Tbsp. snipped fresh dill
   Cooking spray
   Ranch salad dressing,
   optional

1. Preheat air fryer to 400°. Let pickles stand on a paper towel until liquid is almost absorbed, about 15 minutes.

2. Meanwhile, in a shallow bowl, combine flour and salt. In another shallow bowl, whisk eggs, pickle juice, cayenne and garlic powder. Combine panko and dill in a third shallow bowl.

3. Dip pickles in flour mixture to coat both sides; shake off excess. Dip in egg mixture, then in crumb mixture, patting to help coating adhere. In batches, place pickles in a single layer on greased tray in air-fryer basket. Cook until golden brown and crispy, 7-10 minutes. Turn pickles; spritz with cooking spray. Cook until golden brown and crispy, 7-10 minutes longer. Serve immediately. If desired, serve with ranch dressing.

1 pickle slice: 26 cal., 1g fat (0 sat. fat), 13mg chol., 115mg sod., 4g carb. (0 sugars, 0 fiber), 1g pro.

CHEESEBURGER ONION RINGS

This new take on burgers will have your guests begging for seconds. Serve these cheeseburger onion rings with spicy ketchup or your favorite dipping sauce.
—Taste of Home *Test Kitchen*

PREP: 25 MIN. • COOK: 15 MIN./BATCH • MAKES: 8 SERVINGS

1 lb. lean ground
   beef (90% lean)
⅓ cup ketchup
2 Tbsp. prepared mustard
½ tsp. salt
1 large onion
4 oz. cheddar cheese,
   cut into squares
¾ cup all-purpose flour
2 tsp. garlic powder
2 large eggs, lightly beaten
1½ cups panko bread crumbs
   Cooking spray
   Spicy ketchup, optional

1. Preheat air fryer to 335°. In a small bowl, combine beef, ketchup, mustard and salt, mixing lightly but thoroughly. Cut onion into ½-in. slices; separate into rings. Fill 8 rings with half of the beef mixture (save remaining onion rings for another use). Top each with a piece of cheese and remaining beef mixture.

2. In a shallow bowl, mix flour and garlic powder. Place bread crumbs and eggs in separate shallow bowls. Dip filled onion rings in flour to coat both sides; shake off excess. Dip in egg, then in bread crumbs, patting to help coating adhere.

3. In batches, place the onion rings in a single layer on greased tray in air-fryer basket; spritz with cooking spray. Cook until golden brown and a thermometer inserted into beef reads 160°, 12-15 minutes. If desired, serve with spicy ketchup.

1 cheeseburger onion ring: 258 cal., 11g fat (5g sat. fat), 96mg chol., 489mg sod., 19g carb. (4g sugars, 1g fiber), 19g pro.

WHY YOU'LL LOVE IT...
"I have made a different version of these in the past, but this is a better recipe, with the ketchup and mustard flavoring the beef! I added a chopped green chile with the cheese for little kick. For a really good coating, let them rest on a sheet of waxed paper before frying."
—CAST_IRON_KING, TASTEOFHOME.COM

GREEK BREADSTICKS

Get ready for rave reviews. These crisp breadsticks are twisted with Greek-inspired goodness and are best served fresh from the oven.

—Jane Whittaker, Pensacola, FL

PREP: 20 MIN. • COOK: 15 MIN./BATCH • MAKES: 32 BREADSTICKS

¼ cup marinated quartered artichoke hearts, drained
2 Tbsp. pitted Greek olives
1 pkg. (17.3 oz.) frozen puff pastry, thawed
1 carton (6½ oz.) spreadable spinach and artichoke cream cheese
2 Tbsp. grated Parmesan cheese
1 large egg
1 Tbsp. water
2 tsp. sesame seeds
Refrigerated tzatziki sauce, optional

1. Preheat air fryer to 325°. Place artichokes and olives in a food processor; cover and pulse until finely chopped. Unfold 1 pastry sheet on a lightly floured surface; spread half the cream cheese over half of pastry. Top with half the artichoke mixture. Sprinkle with half the Parmesan cheese. Fold plain half over filling; press gently to seal.

2. Repeat with remaining pastry, cream cheese, artichoke mixture and Parmesan cheese. Whisk egg and water; brush over tops. Sprinkle with sesame seeds. Cut each rectangle into sixteen ¾-in.-wide strips. Twist strips several times.

3. In batches, arrange bread sticks in a single layer on greased tray in air-fryer basket. Cook until golden brown, 12-15 minutes. Serve warm with tzatziki sauce if desired.

1 breadstick: 99 cal., 6g fat (2g sat. fat), 11mg chol., 108mg sod., 9g carb. (0 sugars, 1g fiber), 2g pro.

QUENTIN'S PEACH-BOURBON WINGS

My father and husband love bourbon flavor, so I add it to tangy wings air-fried in peach preserves. Stand back and watch these fly off your platter.
—*Christine Winston, Richmond, VA*

PREP: 35 MIN. • COOK: 15 MIN./BATCH • MAKES: ABOUT 1½ DOZEN PIECES

½ cup peach preserves
1 Tbsp. brown sugar
1 garlic cloves, minced
¼ tsp. salt
2 Tbsp. white vinegar
2 Tbsp. bourbon
1 tsp. cornstarch
1½ tsp. water
2 lbs. chicken wings

1. Preheat air fryer to 400°. Place preserves, brown sugar, garlic and salt in a food processor; process until blended. Transfer to a small saucepan. Add the vinegar and bourbon; bring to a boil. Reduce heat; simmer, uncovered, until slightly thickened, 4-6 minutes.

2. In a small bowl, mix cornstarch and water until smooth; stir into the preserves mixture. Return to a boil, stirring constantly; cook and stir 1-2 minutes or until thickened. Reserve ¼ cup sauce for serving.

3. Using a sharp knife, cut through the 2 joints on each chicken wing; discard wing tips. In batches, place wing pieces in a single layer on greased tray in air-fryer basket. Cook 6 minutes; turn and brush with preserves mixture. Cook until browned and juices run clear, 6-8 minutes longer. Serve wings immediately with reserved sauce.

1 piece with about ½ tsp. sauce: 79 cal., 3g fat (1g sat. fat), 15mg chol., 47mg sod., 7g carb. (6g sugars, 0 fiber), 5g pro.

PROSCIUTTO TORTELLINI

This crunchy, gooey-good air-fried tortellini is my take on Italian street food. For the sauce, use the best quality tomato puree you can find.
—*Angela Lemoine, Howell, NJ*

PREP: 25 MIN. • COOK: 10 MIN./BATCH • MAKES: ABOUT 3½ DOZEN

1 Tbsp. olive oil
3 Tbsp. finely chopped onion
4 garlic cloves,
   coarsely chopped
1 can (15 oz.) tomato puree
1 Tbsp. minced fresh basil
¼ tsp. salt
¼ tsp. pepper

TORTELLINI
2 large eggs
2 Tbsp. 2% milk
⅔ cup seasoned bread crumbs
1 tsp. garlic powder
2 Tbsp. grated Pecorino
   Romano cheese
1 Tbsp. minced fresh parsley
½ tsp. salt
1 pkg. (12 oz.) refrigerated
   prosciutto ricotta tortellini
   Cooking spray

1. In a small saucepan, heat oil over medium-high heat. Add onion and garlic; cook and stir until tender, 3-4 minutes. Stir in tomato puree, basil, salt and pepper. Bring to a boil; reduce heat. Simmer, uncovered, 10 minutes. Keep warm.

2. Meanwhile, preheat air fryer to 350°. In a small bowl, whisk eggs and milk. In another bowl, combine bread crumbs, garlic powder, cheese, parsley and salt.

3. Dip tortellini in egg mixture, then in bread crumb mixture to coat. In batches, arrange tortellini in a single layer on greased tray in air-fryer basket; spritz with cooking spray. Cook until golden brown, 4-5 minutes. Turn; spritz with cooking spray. Cook until golden brown, 4-5 minutes longer. Serve with sauce; sprinkle with additional minced fresh basil.

1 appetizer: 38 cal., 1g fat (0 sat. fat), 9mg chol., 96mg sod., 5g carb. (0 sugars, 0 fiber), 1g pro.

FIESTA CHICKEN FINGERS

Chicken fingers have long been a favorite of mine. Actually, almost any finger-shaped deep-fried edible seldom escapes my reach. These air-fryer chicken fingers have taken a lot of the guilt out of my guilty pleasure.
—*Dianne DeGarmo-Carr, Alexander, AR*

PREP: 20 MIN. • COOK: 15 MIN./BATCH • MAKES: 4 SERVINGS

¾ lb. boneless skinless
   chicken breasts
½ cup buttermilk
¼ tsp. pepper
1 cup all-purpose flour
3 cups corn chips, crushed
1 envelope taco seasoning
   Sour cream ranch dip
   or salsa

1. Preheat air fryer to 400°. Pound chicken breasts with a meat mallet to ½-in. thickness. Cut into 1-in. wide strips.

2. In a shallow bowl, whisk buttermilk and pepper. Place flour in a separate shallow bowl. Mix corn chips and taco seasoning in a third bowl. Dip chicken in flour to coat both sides; shake off excess. Dip in buttermilk mixture, then in corn chip mixture, patting to help coating adhere.

3. In batches, arrange chicken in a single layer on greased tray in air-fryer basket; spritz with cooking spray. Cook until coating is golden brown and chicken is no longer pink, 7-8 minutes on each side. Repeat with remaining chicken. Serve with ranch dip or salsa.

1 serving: 676 cal., 36g fat (6g sat. fat), 47mg chol., 1431mg sod., 60g carb. (4g sugars, 3g fiber), 24g pro.

PORTOBELLO MUSHROOM ROLL-UPS

A dish featured on an episode of *Top Chef* was the inspiration behind this party appetizer. I simplified it and tweaked the flavors a bit. The roll-ups, or taquitos, can be made ahead and reheated in a 250° oven for 10 minutes.
—*Lily Julow, Lawrenceville, GA*

PREP: 30 MIN. • COOK: 10 MIN./BATCH • MAKES: 10 SERVINGS

2   Tbsp. extra virgin olive oil
8   oz. large portobello mushrooms, gills discarded, finely chopped
1   tsp. dried oregano
1   tsp. dried thyme
½   tsp. crushed red pepper flakes
¼   tsp. salt
1   pkg. (8 oz.) cream cheese, softened
4   oz. whole-milk ricotta cheese
10 flour tortillas (8 in.)
    Cooking spray
    Chutney

1. In a skillet, heat oil over medium heat. Add mushrooms; saute 4 minutes. Add oregano, thyme, pepper flakes and salt; saute until mushrooms are browned, 4-6 minutes. Cool.

2. Combine cheeses; fold in mushrooms, mixing well. Spread 3 Tbsp. mushroom mixture on bottom-center of each tortilla. Roll up tightly; secure with toothpicks.

3. Preheat air fryer to 400°. In batches, place roll-ups on greased tray in the air-fryer basket; spritz with cooking spray. Cook until golden brown, 9-11 minutes. When roll-ups are cool enough to handle, discard toothpicks. Serve with chutney.

1 appetizer: 291 cal., 16g fat (7g sat. fat), 27mg chol., 380mg sod., 31g carb. (2g sugars, 2g fiber), 8g pro.

TOASTED RAVIOLI

While visiting a friend in St. Louis, I tried toasted ravioli at almost every restaurant we visited. When I got home, I had to replicate them. I think this recipe comes pretty close.
—*Cristina Carrera, Kenosha, WI*

PREP: 20 MIN. • COOK: 10 MIN./BATCH • MAKES: ABOUT 1½ DOZEN

1 cup seasoned bread crumbs
¼ cup shredded
   Parmesan cheese
2 tsp. dried basil
½ cup all-purpose flour
2 large eggs, lightly beaten
1 pkg. (9 oz.) frozen beef
   ravioli, thawed
   Cooking spray
   Fresh minced basil, optional
1 cup marinara
   sauce, warmed

1. Preheat air fryer to 350°. In a shallow bowl, mix bread crumbs, Parmesan cheese and basil. Place flour and eggs in separate shallow bowls. Dip ravioli in flour to coat both sides; shake off excess. Dip in eggs, then in crumb mixture, patting to help coating adhere.

2. In batches, arrange ravioli in a single layer on greased tray in air-fryer basket; spritz with cooking spray. Cook until golden brown, 3-4 minutes. Turn; spritz with cooking spray. Cook until golden brown, 3-4 minutes longer. If desired, immediately sprinkle with basil and additional Parmesan cheese. Serve warm with marinara sauce.

1 piece: 40 cal., 1g fat (0 sat. fat), 6mg chol., 117mg sod., 6g carb. (1g sugars, 1g fiber), 2g pro.

CHICKPEA FRITTERS WITH SWEET-SPICY SAUCE

Chickpeas are a common ingredient in many dishes in Pakistan where I grew up. I incorporate the tastes of my home country when cooking for my American-born daughters. Here I combined the light spice of Pakistani foods with the love of deep-fried foods that many Americans, including my daughters, enjoy. To eat, dip the warm fritters in the chilled yogurt. Enjoy as a snack, appetizer, or as part of a meal.
—*Shahrin Hasan, York, PA*

PREP: 20 MIN. • COOK: 5 MIN./BATCH • MAKES: 2 DOZEN (1 CUP SAUCE)

1   cup plain yogurt
2   Tbsp. sugar
1   Tbsp. honey
½   tsp. salt
½   tsp. pepper
½   tsp. crushed red
    pepper flakes

FRITTERS
1   can (15 oz.) chickpeas
    or garbanzo beans,
    rinsed and drained
1   tsp. ground cumin
½   tsp. salt
½   tsp. garlic powder
½   tsp. ground ginger
1   large egg
½   tsp. baking soda
½   cup chopped fresh cilantro
2   green onions, thinly sliced

1. Preheat air-fryer to 400°. In a small bowl, combine the first 6 ingredients; refrigerate until serving.

2. Place chickpeas and seasonings in a food processor; process until finely ground. Add egg and baking soda; pulse until blended. Transfer to a bowl; stir in cilantro and green onions.

3. In batches, drop rounded tablespoons of bean mixture onto greased tray in air-fryer basket. Cook until lightly browned, 5-6 minutes. Serve with sauce.

1 fritter with 2 tsp. sauce: 34 cal., 1g fat (0 sat. fat), 9mg chol., 156mg sod., 5g carb. (3g sugars, 1g fiber), 1g pro.

CRISPY POTATO CHIPS

I received an air fryer for Christmas one year. Crispy potato chips are an essential part of any good lunch, so I decided to use my new appliance to make a guilt-free version. They turned out delicious, and just like the bagged kind, you won't be able to stop at just one.

—Melissa Obernesser, Utica, NY

PREP: 30 MIN. • COOK: 15 MIN./BATCH • MAKES: 6 SERVINGS

2 large potatoes
Olive oil-flavored
cooking spray
½ tsp. sea salt
Minced fresh parsley,
optional

1. Preheat air fryer to 360°. Using a mandoline or vegetable peeler, cut potatoes into very thin slices. Transfer to a large bowl; add enough ice water to cover. Soak for 15 minutes; drain. Add ice water again and soak for 15 minutes.

2. Drain potatoes; place on towels and pat dry. Spritz potatoes with cooking spray; sprinkle with salt. In batches, place potato slices in a single layer on tray in greased air-fryer basket. Cook until crisp and golden brown, 15-17 minutes, stirring and turning every 5-7 minutes. If desired, sprinkle with parsley.

1 cup: 148 cal., 1g fat (0 sat. fat), 0 chol., 252mg sod., 32g carb. (2g sugars, 4g fiber), 4g pro. **Diabetic exchanges:** 2 starch.

ROSEMARY SAUSAGE MEATBALLS

These air-fryer meatballs were created as hors d'oeuvres for a friend's wedding and became an instant hit. Now we enjoy them often at our house.
—*Steve Hansen, Redmond, WA*

PREP: 20 MIN. • COOK: 10 MIN./BATCH • MAKES: ABOUT 2 DOZEN

2 Tbsp. olive oil
4 garlic cloves, minced
1 tsp. curry powder
1 large egg, lightly beaten
1 jar (4 oz.) diced pimientos, drained
¼ cup dry bread crumbs
¼ cup minced fresh parsley
1 Tbsp. minced fresh rosemary
2 lbs. bulk pork sausage
    Pretzel sticks, optional

1. Preheat air fryer to 400°. In a small skillet, heat oil over medium heat; saute garlic with curry powder until tender, 1-2 minutes. Cool slightly.

2. In a bowl, combine egg, pimientos, bread crumbs, parsley, rosemary and garlic mixture. Add sausage; mix lightly but thoroughly.

3. Shape into 1¼-in. balls. Place in a single layer on tray in air-fryer basket; cook until lightly browned and cooked through, 7-10 minutes. If desired, serve with pretzels.

1 meatball: 96 cal., 8g fat (2g sat. fat), 24mg chol., 208mg sod., 2g carb. (0 sugars, 0 fiber), 4g pro.

WASABI CRAB CAKES

With wasabi in both the crab cakes and the dipping sauce, this festive appetizer brings its own heat to the party.
—*Marie Rizzio, Interlochen, MI*

PREP: 20 MIN. • COOK: 10 MIN./BATCH • MAKES: 2 DOZEN (½ CUP SAUCE)

1   medium sweet red
    pepper, finely chopped
1   celery rib, finely chopped
3   green onions,
    finely chopped
2   large egg whites
3   Tbsp. reduced-fat
    mayonnaise
¼   tsp. prepared wasabi
¼   tsp. salt
⅓   cup plus ½ cup dry
    bread crumbs, divided
1½ cups lump crabmeat,
    drained
    Cooking spray

SAUCE
1   celery rib, chopped
⅓   cup reduced-fat
    mayonnaise
1   green onion, chopped
1   Tbsp. sweet pickle relish
½   tsp. prepared wasabi
¼   tsp. celery salt

1. Preheat air fryer to 375°. Combine first 7 ingredients; add ⅓ cup bread crumbs. Gently fold in crab.

2. Place the remaining bread crumbs in a shallow bowl. Drop heaping tablespoons of crab mixture into crumbs. Gently coat and shape into ¾-in.-thick patties. In batches, place the crab cakes in a single layer on greased tray in air-fryer basket. Spritz crab cakes with cooking spray. Cook until golden brown, 8-12 minutes, carefully turning halfway through cooking and spritzing with additional cooking spray.

3. Meanwhile, place sauce ingredients in food processor; pulse 2 or 3 times to blend or until desired consistency is reached. Serve crab cakes immediately with dipping sauce.

1 crab cake with 1 tsp. sauce: 49 cal., 2g fat (0 sat. fat), 13mg chol., 179mg sod., 4g carb. (1g sugars, 0 fiber), 3g pro.

BEEF WELLINGTON WONTONS

Try this tasty riff on classic beef Wellingtons. The scaled-down bites are the ideal size to include in a lineup of fun and fancy finger foods of all kinds.
—*Dianne Phillips, Tallapoosa, GA*

PREP: 35 MIN. • COOK: 10 MIN./BATCH • MAKES: 3½ DOZEN

½ lb. lean ground beef (90% lean)
1 Tbsp. butter
1 Tbsp. olive oil
2 garlic cloves, minced
1½ tsp. chopped shallot
1 cup each chopped fresh shiitake, baby portobello and white mushrooms
¼ cup dry red wine
1 Tbsp. minced fresh parsley
½ tsp. salt
¼ tsp. pepper
1 pkg. (12 oz.) wonton wrappers
1 large egg
1 Tbsp. water
Cooking spray

1. Preheat air fryer to 325°. In a small skillet, cook ground beef over medium heat until no longer pink, breaking into crumbles, 4-5 minutes; transfer to a large bowl. In the same skillet, heat butter and olive oil over medium-high heat. Add the garlic and shallot; cook 1 minute. Stir in mushrooms and wine. Cook until mushrooms are tender, 8-10 minutes; add to beef. Stir in the parsley, salt and pepper.

2. Place about 2 tsp. filling in the center of each wonton wrapper. Combine the egg and water. Moisten wonton edges with egg mixture; fold opposite corners over filling and press to seal.

Freeze option: Cover unbaked wontons on parchment-lined baking sheets and freeze until firm. Transfer to airtight freezer containers; return to freezer. To use, cook pastries as directed.

1 wonton: 42 cal., 1g fat (0 sat. fat), 9mg chol., 82mg sod., 5g carb. (0 sugars, 0 fiber), 2g pro.

SPRING ROLLS WITH SRIRACHA

While vacationing in the Bahamas, I dined at a restaurant that served the most amazing chicken spring rolls. When got home, I created my own version. These are a fantastic appetizer—whether you enjoy them right away or stash some in the freezer to enjoy later!
—*Carla Mendres, Winnipeg, MB*

PREP: 50 MIN. • COOK: 10 MIN./BATCH • MAKES: 2 DOZEN

3 cups coleslaw mix (about 7 oz.)
3 green onions, chopped
1 Tbsp. soy sauce
1 tsp. sesame oil
1 lb. boneless skinless chicken breasts
1 tsp. seasoned salt
2 pkg. (8 oz. each) cream cheese, softened
2 Tbsp. Sriracha chili sauce
24 spring roll wrappers
 Cooking spray
 Sweet chili sauce, optional

1. Preheat air fryer to 360°. Toss coleslaw mix, green onions, soy sauce and sesame oil; let stand while cooking chicken. Place chicken in a single layer on greased tray in air-fryer basket. Cook until a thermometer inserted in chicken reads 165°, 18-20 minutes. Remove chicken and cool slightly. Finely chop chicken; toss with seasoned salt.

2. Increase air-fryer temperature to 400°. In a large bowl, mix the cream cheese and Sriracha chili sauce; stir in chicken and coleslaw mixture. With 1 corner of a spring roll wrapper facing you, place about 2 Tbsp. filling just below center of wrapper. (Cover remaining wrappers with a damp paper towel until ready to use.) Fold bottom corner over filling; moisten remaining edges with water. Fold side corners toward center over filling; roll up tightly, pressing tip to seal. Repeat.

Freeze option: Freeze uncooked spring rolls 1 in. apart in freezer containers, separating layers with waxed paper. To use, cook frozen spring rolls as directed, increasing time as necessary.

1 spring roll: 127 cal., 7g fat (4g sat. fat), 30mg chol., 215mg sod., 10g carb. (1g sugars, 0 fiber), 6g pro.

SUN-DRIED TOMATO GOAT CHEESE EMPANADAS

I entertain a lot, so I appreciate make-ahead recipes. These hand-held bites are easy and delicious. I recommend making a few extra batches—they go fast!
—Lynn Scully, Rancho Santa Fe, CA

PREP: 1 HOUR • COOK: 10 MIN./BATCH • MAKES: ABOUT 1½ DOZEN

1   Tbsp. olive oil
1   medium sweet onion, halved and thinly sliced
1   log (4 oz.) fresh goat cheese, crumbled
¼   cup finely chopped oil-packed sun-dried tomatoes, drained
    Pastry for a single-crust pie or refrigerated pie crust
    Cooking spray

1. In a large skillet, heat olive oil over medium heat. Add onion; cook and stir until softened, 4-5 minutes. Reduce the heat to medium-low; cook, stirring occasionally, until deep golden brown, 30-40 minutes. Remove from heat. Let cool slightly. Gently stir in goat cheese and tomatoes.

2. Preheat air fryer to 375°. On a lightly floured surface, roll dough to ¼-in. thickness. Cut with a floured 3-in. round biscuit cutter. Place 1 heaping tsp. filling on 1 side of each circle. Brush edges of pastry with water; fold circles in half. With a fork, press edges to seal.

3. In batches, arrange empanadas in a single layer on greased tray in air-fryer basket; spritz with cooking spray. Cook until golden brown, 4-5 minutes. Turn; spritz with cooking spray. Cook until golden brown, 4-5 minutes longer.

1 empanada: 99 cal., 7g fat (4g sat. fat), 18mg chol., 98mg sod., 8g carb. (0 sugars, 0 fiber), 2g pro.

CHAPTER 2

BREAKFAST & BRUNCH

Your cool new kitchen gadget isn't just for savory party snacks. Turn to it in the early hours of the day to create a delicious and filling meal that will keep you energized. Whether you fancy bite-sized ham and cheese bundles, a big iced cinnamon roll or a new take on French toast, you'll have no trouble finding your new favorite breakfast!

HAM & EGG POCKETS

Fans of hand-held pies and frozen pockets will appreciate these savory air-fryer breakfast treats. Refrigerated crescent roll dough makes them a snap to prepare.
—Taste of Home *Test Kitchen*

TAKES: 25 MIN. • MAKES: 2 SERVINGS

1 large egg
2 tsp. 2% milk
2 tsp. butter
1 oz. thinly sliced deli ham, chopped
2 Tbsp. shredded cheddar cheese
1 tube (4 oz.) refrigerated crescent rolls

1. Preheat air fryer to 300°. In a small bowl, combine egg and milk. In a small skillet heat butter until hot. Add egg mixture; cook and stir over medium heat until eggs are completely set. Remove from the heat. Fold in ham and cheese.

2. Separate crescent dough into 2 rectangles. Seal perforations; spoon half the filling down the center of each rectangle. Fold the dough over filling and pinch to seal. Place in a single layer on greased tray in air-fryer basket. Cook until golden brown, 8-10 minutes.

1 pocket: 326 cal., 20g fat (5g sat. fat), 118mg chol., 735mg sod., 25g carb. (6g sugars, 0 fiber), 12g pro.

BOURBON BACON CINNAMON ROLLS

This recipe is the perfect combination of savory and sweet. The bourbon-soaked bacon adds a smoky, savory, bold taste to cinnamon rolls. The ginger and pecan topping makes for a crunchy, spicy finish.
—*Shannen Casey, Citrus Heights, CA*

PREP: 25 MIN. + MARINATING • COOK: 10 MIN./BATCH • MAKES: 8 ROLLS

8   bacon strips
¾   cup bourbon
1   tube (12.4 oz.) refrigerated cinnamon rolls with icing
½   cup chopped pecans
2   Tbsp. maple syrup
1   tsp. minced fresh gingerroot

1. Place bacon in a shallow dish; add bourbon. Cover and seal; refrigerate overnight. Remove the bacon and pat dry; discard bourbon.

2. In a large skillet, cook bacon in batches over medium heat until nearly crisp but still pliable. Remove the bacon to paper towels to drain. Discard all but 1 tsp. drippings.

3. Preheat air fryer to 350°. Separate the dough into 8 rolls, reserving icing packet. Unroll spiral rolls into long strips; pat dough to form 6x1-in. strips. Place 1 bacon strip on each strip of dough, trimming bacon as needed; reroll, forming a spiral. Pinch ends to seal. Repeat with the remaining dough. Place 4 rolls on ungreased tray in air-fryer basket; cook 5 minutes. Turn rolls over and cook until golden brown, about 4 minutes.

4. Meanwhile, combine pecans and maple syrup. In another bowl, stir ginger with contents of icing packet. In same skillet, heat remaining bacon drippings over medium heat. Add the pecan mixture; cook, stirring frequently, until lightly toasted, 2-3 minutes.

5. Drizzle half the icing over warm cinnamon rolls; top with half the pecans. Repeat to make a second batch.

1 roll: 267 cal., 14g fat (3g sat. fat), 9mg chol., 490mg sod., 28g carb. (13g sugars, 1g fiber), 5g pro.

HAM & CHEESE BREAKFAST BUNDLES

My family looks forward to these rich and delicious egg bundles. They're perfect for holidays, brunches and birthdays. Thanks to air-frying, they're fast, too!
—Cindy Bride, Bloomfield, IA

PREP: 35 MIN. • COOK: 10 MIN. • MAKES: 4 SERVINGS

5 sheets phyllo dough (14x9 in.)
¼ cup butter, melted
2 oz. cream cheese, cut into 4 pieces
4 large eggs
⅛ tsp. salt
⅛ tsp. pepper
¼ cup chopped fully cooked ham
¼ cup shredded provolone cheese
2 tsp. seasoned bread crumbs
2 tsp. minced chives

1. Preheat air fryer to 325°. Place 1 sheet of phyllo dough on a work surface; brush with butter. Layer with 4 additional phyllo sheets, brushing each layer. (Keep the remaining phyllo covered with a damp towel to keep it from drying out.) Cut layered sheets crosswise in half, then lengthwise in half.

2. Place each stack in a greased 4-oz. ramekin. Fill each with a piece of cream cheese. Carefully break an egg into each cup. Sprinkle with salt and pepper; top with the ham, cheese, bread crumbs and chives. Bring phyllo together above filling; pinch to seal and form bundles.

3. Place ramekins on tray in air-fryer basket; brush with remaining butter. Cook until golden brown, 10-12 minutes. Serve warm.

1 bundle: 301 cal., 24g fat (13g sat. fat), 241mg chol., 522mg sod., 10g carb. (1g sugars, 0 fiber), 12g pro.

BREAKFAST COOKIES

Cookies for breakfast? Yes, please! I used to buy the expensive brand-name kind from the supermarket, but ever since I found this recipe, I've had fun making my own. As an added bonus, these are loaded with good-for-you ingredients.

—*Linda Burciaga*, tasteofhome.com

PREP: 20 MIN. • COOK: 10 MIN./BATCH • MAKES: 1 DOZEN

1 cup mashed ripe bananas (about 2 medium)
½ cup chunky peanut butter
½ cup honey
1 tsp. vanilla extract
1 cup old-fashioned oats
½ cup whole wheat flour
¼ cup nonfat dry milk powder
2 tsp. ground cinnamon
½ tsp. salt
¼ tsp. baking soda
1 cup dried cranberries or raisins

1. Preheat air fryer to 300°. Beat banana, peanut butter, honey and vanilla until blended. In another bowl, combine oats, flour, milk powder, cinnamon, salt and baking soda; gradually beat into banana mixture. Stir in dried cranberries.

2. In batches, drop dough by ¼ cupfuls 2 in. apart onto greased tray in air-fryer basket; flatten to ½-in. thickness.

3. Cook until lightly browned, 6-8 minutes. Cool in basket 1 minute. Remove to wire racks.

4. Serve warm or at room temperature.

Freeze option: Freeze cookies in freezer containers, separating layers with waxed paper. To use, thaw before serving or, if desired, reheat in a preheated 300° air fryer until warmed, about 1 minute.

1 cookie: 212 cal., 6g fat (1g sat. fat), 0 chol., 186mg sod., 38g carb. (25g sugars, 4g fiber), 5g pro.

BACON CRESCENT ROLLS

The mouthwatering aroma of these easy three-ingredient crescents will draw folks to the table. Kids can join in the fun of assembly—let them unroll the dough and sprinkle the triangles with the onion powder and cooled bacon crumbles.

—Jane Nearing, Indianapolis, IN

PREP: 10 MIN. • COOK: 10 MIN./BATCH • MAKES: 8 SERVINGS

1 tube (8 oz.) refrigerated crescent rolls
6 bacon strips, cooked and crumbled
1 tsp. onion powder

Preheat air fryer to 300°. Unroll crescent dough and separate into 8 triangles. Set aside 1 Tbsp. of bacon. Sprinkle the onion powder and remaining bacon over triangles. Roll up and sprinkle with remaining bacon, pressing lightly to adhere.

Freeze option: Freeze cooled rolls in freezer containers. To use, thaw at room temperature or, if desired, microwave each roll on high until heated through, 10-15 seconds.

1 roll: 133 cal., 7g fat (1g sat. fat), 6mg chol., 322mg sod., 12g carb. (3g sugars, 0 fiber), 4g pro.

BREAKFAST CROQUETTES WITH EGG & ASPARAGUS

I was in search of a new breakfast I could grab on the run and I liked the idea of combining different flavors, so I created these egg roll-like croquettes. If you want to get fancy, sprinkle them with paprika and serve with hollandaise sauce.
—*Barbara Miller, Oakdale, MN*

PREP: 30 MIN. + CHILLING • COOK: 15 MIN./BATCH • MAKES: 6 SERVINGS

3   Tbsp. butter
3   Tbsp. all-purpose flour
¾   cup 2% milk
6   hard-boiled large
     eggs, chopped
½   cup chopped fresh
     asparagus
½   cup chopped green onions
⅓   cup shredded
     cheddar cheese
1   Tbsp. minced fresh
     tarragon
¼   tsp. salt
¼   tsp. pepper
1¾ cups panko bread crumbs
3   large eggs, beaten
     Cooking spray

1. In a large saucepan, melt the butter over medium heat. Stir in flour until smooth; cook and stir until lightly browned, 1-2 minutes. Gradually whisk in milk; cook and stir until thickened (mixture will be thick). Stir in hard-boiled eggs, asparagus, green onions, cheese, tarragon, salt and pepper. Refrigerate at least 2 hours.

2. Preheat air fryer to 350°. Shape ¼ cupfuls of egg mixture into twelve 3-in. long ovals. Place bread crumbs and eggs in separate shallow bowls. Roll logs in crumbs to coat, then dip in egg and roll again in crumbs, patting to help coating adhere.

3. In batches, place croquettes in a single layer on greased tray in air-fryer basket; spritz with cooking spray. Cook until golden brown, 8-10 minutes. Turn; spritz with cooking spray. Cook until golden brown, 3-5 minutes longer.

2 croquettes: 294 cal., 17g fat (8g sat. fat), 303mg chol., 348mg sod., 18g carb. (3g sugars, 1g fiber), 15g pro.

FRENCH TOAST STICKS

Make French toast sticks that rival any restaurant or store-bought version with this quick and easy recipe. I like to have them handy in the freezer for a hearty meal in an instant. They're great for everything from formal brunch buffets to lazy weekend breakfasts with the kids.
—Taste of Home *Test Kitchen*

PREP: 20 MIN. + FREEZING • COOK: 10 MIN. • MAKES: 1½ DOZEN

6 slices day-old Texas toast
4 large eggs
1 cup whole milk
2 Tbsp. sugar
1 tsp. vanilla extract
¼ to ½ tsp. ground cinnamon
1 cup crushed
    cornflakes, optional
    Confectioners' sugar,
    optional
    Maple syrup

1. Cut each piece of bread into thirds; place in an ungreased 13x9-in. dish. In a large bowl, whisk eggs, milk, sugar, vanilla and cinnamon. Pour over bread; soak for 2 minutes, turning once. If desired, coat bread with cornflake crumbs on all sides.

2. Place in a greased 15x10x1-in. baking pan. Freeze until firm, about 45 minutes. Remove sticks from the freezer to cook or transfer to an airtight container and store in the freezer.

3. When ready to cook, preheat air fryer to 350°. Place desired number on greased tray in air-fryer basket. Cook for 3 minutes. Turn; cook until golden brown, 2-3 minutes longer. Sprinkle with confectioners' sugar if desired. Serve with syrup.

3 sticks: 184 cal., 6g fat (2g sat. fat), 128mg chol., 253mg sod., 24g carb. (8g sugars, 1g fiber), 8g pro.

WHY YOU'LL LOVE IT...
"Easy, quick and gone in the wink of an eye. My kids love to dip them in syrup, but of course they love anything they can eat with their hands."
—RODRICAT, TASTEOFHOME.COM

TOAD-IN-THE-HOLE

Toad-in-the-Hole is a British comfort food dish consisting of sausages baked in Yorkshire pudding. It's commonly served at suppertime, but we enjoy it for breakfast. No matter the time of day, it's guaranteed to be a favorite in your house, too.
—*Leigh Rys, Herndon, VA*

PREP: 10 MIN. • COOK: 25 MIN. • MAKES: 4 SERVINGS

8 frozen turkey breakfast sausage links
2 large eggs
1 cup 2% milk
½ cup all-purpose flour
1 tsp. onion powder
1 tsp. stone-ground mustard
⅛ tsp. salt
⅛ tsp. pepper
Optional: 1 bacon strip, cooked and crumbled, and minced parsley

1. Preheat air fryer to 400°. Cut the sausages in half widthwise. Arrange in a greased 6-in. round baking pan. Place pan on tray in air-fryer basket. Cook until lightly browned, 6-8 minutes, turning once.

2. Meanwhile, in a large bowl, whisk eggs, milk, flour, onion powder, mustard, salt, and pepper. If desired, stir in bacon; pour over sausages. Cook until puffed and golden brown, 10-15 minutes. Serve immediately and, if desired, garnish with parsley.

1 serving: 257 cal., 15g fat (5g sat. fat), 143mg chol., 494mg sod., 16g carb. (3g sugars, 1g fiber), 16g pro.

DOUGHNUT HOLES WITH NUTELLA

Convenient refrigerated biscuits make these sugar-dusted breakfast bites a snap to prepare. You can cut and assemble the doughnut holes in advance and refrigerate. Just be sure to bring the dough to room temperature before frying.
—*Renee Murphy, Smithtown, NY*

PREP: 30 MIN. • COOK: 5 MIN./BATCH • MAKES: 32 DOUGHNUTS

1 large egg
1 Tbsp. water
1 tube (16.3 oz.) large refrigerated flaky biscuits (8 count)
⅔ cup Nutella
Oil for deep-fat frying
Confectioners' sugar

1. Preheat air fryer to 300°. Whisk egg with water. On a lightly floured surface, roll each biscuit into a 6-in. circle; cut each into 4 wedges. Brush lightly with egg mixture; top each wedge with 1 tsp. Nutella. Bring up corners over filling; pinch edges firmly to seal.

2. In batches, arrange biscuits in a single layer on ungreased tray in air-fryer basket. Cook until golden brown, 8-10 minutes, turning once. Dust with confectioners' sugar; serve warm.

1 doughnut: 94 cal., 6g fat (1g sat. fat), 6mg chol., 119mg sod., 10g carb. (4g sugars, 0 fiber), 1g pro.

CHEESY BREAKFAST EGG ROLLS

When my kids were growing up, it seemed as if we were always grabbing breakfast and running out the door. This recipe is perfect for busy days like that, but also good for those times you want to leisurely enjoy your morning meal. Either way, these are sure to be a hit!
—*Anne Ormond, Dover, NH*

PREP: 30 MIN. • COOK: 10 MIN./BATCH • MAKES: 12 SERVINGS

½ lb. bulk pork sausage
½ cup shredded sharp cheddar cheese
½ cup shredded Monterey Jack cheese
1 Tbsp. chopped green onions
4 large eggs
1 Tbsp. 2% milk
¼ tsp. salt
⅛ tsp. pepper
1 Tbsp. butter
12 egg roll wrappers
Maple syrup or salsa, optional

1. In a small nonstick skillet, cook sausage over medium heat until no longer pink, 4-6 minutes, breaking into crumbles; drain. Stir in cheeses and green onions; set aside. Wipe skillet clean.

2. In a small bowl, whisk the eggs, milk, salt and pepper until blended. In the same skillet, heat the butter over medium heat. Pour in egg mixture; cook and stir until eggs are thickened and no liquid egg remains. Stir in sausage mixture.

3. Preheat the air fryer to 400°. With 1 corner of an egg roll wrapper facing you, place ¼ cup filling just below the center of wrapper. (Cover remaining wrappers with a damp paper towel until ready to use.) Fold the bottom corner over filling; moisten remaining wrapper edges with water. Fold the side corners toward center over filling. Roll egg roll up tightly, pressing at tip to seal. Repeat.

4. In batches, arrange egg rolls in a single layer on greased tray in air-fryer basket; spritz with cooking spray. Cook until lightly browned, 3-4 minutes. Turn; spritz with cooking spray. Cook until golden brown and crisp, 3-4 minutes longer. If desired, serve with maple syrup or salsa.

1 egg roll: 209 cal., 10g fat (4g sat. fat), 87mg chol., 438mg sod., 19g carb. (0 sugars, 1g fiber), 10g pro.

PUFF PASTRY DANISHES

Even though they're simple to make, these petite jam-filled pastries are right at home in a classy brunch spread. They were my dad's favorite, so the recipe will always be close to my heart.
—*Chellis Richardson, Jackson Center, OH*

PREP: 25 MIN. • COOK: 10 MIN./BATCH • MAKES: 1½ DOZEN

1 pkg. (8 oz.) cream cheese, softened
¼ cup sugar
2 Tbsp. all-purpose flour
½ tsp. vanilla extract
2 large egg yolks
1 Tbsp. water
1 pkg. (17.3 oz.) frozen puff pastry, thawed
⅔ cup seedless raspberry jam or jam of choice

1. Preheat air fryer to 325°. Beat cream cheese, sugar, flour and vanilla until smooth; beat in 1 egg yolk.

2. Mix water and remaining egg yolk. On a lightly floured surface, unfold each sheet of puff pastry; roll into a 12-in. square. Cut each into nine 4-in. squares.

3. Top each square with 1 Tbsp. cream cheese mixture and 1 rounded tsp. jam. Bring 2 opposite corners of pastry over filling, sealing with yolk mixture. Brush tops with the remaining yolk mixture.

4. In batches, place in a single layer on greased tray in air-fryer basket. Cook until golden brown, 8-10 minutes. Serve warm. Refrigerate leftovers.

1 pastry: 197 cal., 12g fat (4g sat. fat), 33mg chol., 130mg sod., 20g carb. (3g sugars, 2g fiber), 3g pro.

RASPBERRY FRENCH TOAST CUPS

A delightful twist on French toast, these individual treats make any morning special.
I made this recipe for my mom on Mother's Day one year, and we both enjoyed it.
—*Sandi Tuttle, Hayward, WI*

PREP: 20 MIN. + CHILLING • COOK: 20 MIN. • MAKES: 2 SERVINGS

2 slices Italian bread,
   cut into ½-in. cubes
½ cup fresh or frozen
   raspberries
2 oz. cream cheese, cut
   into ½-in. cubes
2 large eggs
½ cup whole milk
1 Tbsp. maple syrup

RASPBERRY SYRUP
2 tsp. cornstarch
⅓ cup water
2 cups fresh or frozen
   raspberries, divided
1 Tbsp. lemon juice
1 Tbsp. maple syrup
½ tsp. grated lemon zest
   Ground cinnamon, optional

1. Divide half the bread cubes between 2 greased 8-oz. custard cups. Sprinkle with raspberries and cream cheese. Top with remaining bread. In a small bowl, whisk the eggs, milk and syrup; pour over bread. Cover and refrigerate for at least 1 hour.

2. Preheat air fryer to 325°. Place the custard cups on tray in air-fryer basket. Cook until golden brown and puffed, 12-15 minutes.

3. Meanwhile, in a small saucepan, combine cornstarch and water until smooth. Add 1½ cups raspberries, lemon juice, syrup and lemon zest. Bring to a boil; reduce heat. Cook and stir until thickened, about 2 minutes. Strain and discard raspberry seeds; cool slightly.

4. Gently stir remaining ½ cup berries into syrup. If desired, sprinkle French toast cups with cinnamon; serve with syrup.

1 serving: 406 cal., 18g fat (8g sat. fat), 221mg chol., 301mg sod., 50g carb. (24g sugars, 11g fiber), 14g pro.

CHAPTER 3

SIDE DISHES

A meal isn't complete without tantalizing sides to enhance the main dish. Tonight, think beyond the standard scoop of mashed potatoes and get creative with one of these air-fried accompaniments. Not only does this handy appliance make delicious dinner sidekicks, it saves space on the stovetop and in the oven, too.

LEMON-PARMESAN ASPARAGUS

These spears are packed with flavor, thanks to the lemon-garlic dressing they're tossed in before cooking. It's a simple, quick side that goes with almost any main dish.

—*Tina Mirilovich, Johnstown, PA*

TAKES: 20 MIN. • MAKES: 4 SERVINGS

¼ cup mayonnaise
4 tsp. olive oil
1½ tsp. grated lemon zest
1 garlic clove, minced
½ tsp. pepper
¼ tsp. seasoned salt
1 lb. fresh asparagus, trimmed
2 Tbsp. shredded Parmesan cheese
Lemon wedges, optional

1. Preheat air fryer to 375°. In large bowl, combine the first 6 ingredients. Add asparagus; toss to coat. In batches, place in a single layer on greased tray in air-fryer basket.

2. Cook until tender and lightly browned, 4-6 minutes. Transfer to a serving platter; sprinkle with Parmesan cheese. If desired, serve with lemon wedges.

1 serving: 156 cal., 15g fat (3g sat. fat), 3mg chol., 214mg sod., 3g carb. (1g sugars, 1g fiber), 2g pro. **Diabetic exchanges:** 3 fat, 1 vegetable.

TEST KITCHEN TIP: When buying asparagus, look for firm, straight, uniform-size spears. The tips should be closed and dry. To keep asparagus fresh longer, place the cut stems in a container of cold water—similar to flowers in a vase. Place the container in the refrigerator, changing the water at least once every 2 days.

ITALIAN BREAD SALAD WITH OLIVES

This Mediterranean-inspired salad always gets rave reviews from my friends and family. It's can be made ahead, so it's a timesaver during the holidays.
—*Angela Spengler, Niceville, FL*

TAKES: 25 MIN. • MAKES: 4 SERVINGS

5 cups cubed ciabatta bread (½-in. cubes)
⅓ cup olive oil
1 garlic clove, minced
⅛ tsp. pepper
2 Tbsp. balsamic vinegar
⅛ tsp. salt
1 large tomato, chopped
2 Tbsp. sliced ripe olives
2 Tbsp. coarsely chopped fresh basil
1 Tbsp. chopped fresh Italian parsley
2 Tbsp. shredded Parmesan cheese

1. Preheat air fryer to 350°. Place bread cubes in a large bowl. In another bowl, mix oil, garlic and pepper; drizzle 2 Tbsp. over bread and toss to coat. Reserve remaining oil mixture.

2. Pace bread cubes on greased tray in air-fryer basket. Cook until crisp and light brown, 7-9 minutes, stirring occasionally.

3. Meanwhile, whisk vinegar and salt into reserved oil mixture. Add tomatoes, olives and herbs; toss to coat. Cool bread cubes slightly. Add to tomato mixture; toss to combine. Sprinkle with cheese; serve immediately.

1 cup: 308 cal., 21g fat (3g sat. fat), 2mg chol., 365mg sod., 26g carb. (6g sugars, 2g fiber), 5g pro.

PUMPKIN FRIES

Move over French fries! These homemade pumpkin fries taste divine and are healthier than their traditional counterpart. They are simple to make and crisp up beautifully in the air fryer. The maple-chipotle dipping sauce is the perfect accompaniment.

—Julie Peterson, Crofton, MD

PREP: 25 MIN. • COOK: 15 MIN./BATCH • MAKES: 4 SERVINGS

½ cup plain Greek yogurt
2 Tbsp. maple syrup
2 to 3 tsp. minced chipotle peppers in adobo sauce
⅛ tsp. plus ½ tsp. salt, divided
1 medium pie pumpkin
¼ tsp. garlic powder
¼ tsp. ground cumin
¼ tsp. chili powder
¼ tsp. pepper

1. In a small bowl, combine yogurt, maple syrup, chipotle peppers and ⅛ tsp. salt. Refrigerate, covered, until serving.

2. Preheat air fryer to 400°. Peel pumpkin; cut in half lengthwise. Discard seeds or save for toasting. Cut into ½-in. strips. Transfer to a large bowl. Sprinkle with the remaining ½ tsp. salt, garlic powder, cumin, chili powder and pepper; toss to coat.

3. In batches, arrange pumpkin on greased tray in air-fryer basket. Cook until just tender, 6-8 minutes. Toss to redistribute; cook until browned and crisp, 3-5 minutes longer. Serve with sauce.

½ cup pumpkin fries with 2 Tbsp. sauce: 151 cal., 3g fat (2g sat. fat), 8mg chol., 413mg sod., 31g carb. (12g sugars, 2g fiber), 5g pro.

TEST KITCHEN TIP: If you don't have pumpkin on hand, butternut squash makes an excellent substitute. And don't forget to save those seeds for roasting!

ROASTED GREEN BEANS

Our family loves roasted green beans, but they can take a long time in the oven.
I tried these out in our air fryer and we loved them!
—*Courtney Stultz, Weir, KS*

PREP: 15 MIN. • COOK: 20 MIN. • MAKES: 6 SERVINGS

1   lb. fresh green beans,
    cut into 2-in. pieces
½   lb. sliced fresh mushrooms
1   small red onion, halved
    and thinly sliced
2   Tbsp. olive oil
1   tsp. Italian seasoning
¼   tsp. salt
⅛   tsp. pepper

1. Preheat air fryer to 375°. In a large bowl, combine all ingredients; toss to coat.

2. Arrange vegetables on greased tray in air-fryer basket. Cook until just tender, 8-10 minutes. Toss to redistribute; cook until browned, 8-10 minutes longer.

⅔ **cup:** 76 cal., 5g fat (1g sat. fat), 0 chol., 105mg sod., 8g carb. (3g sugars, 3g fiber), 3g pro. **Diabetic exchanges:** 1 vegetable, 1 fat.

GARLIC-ROSEMARY BRUSSELS SPROUTS

This is my go-to Thanksgiving side dish. It's healthy, easy and doesn't take much time or effort to make. I usually use rosemary for my turkey so this lets me use up some of the leftover herbs.
—*Elisabeth Larsen, Pleasant Grove, UT*

TAKES: 30 MIN. • MAKES: 4 SERVINGS

3 Tbsp. olive oil
2 garlic cloves, minced
½ tsp. salt
¼ tsp. pepper
1 lb. Brussels sprouts, trimmed and halved
½ cup panko bread crumbs
1½ tsp. minced fresh rosemary

1. Preheat air fryer to 350°. Place first 4 ingredients in a small microwave-safe bowl; microwave on high 30 seconds.

2. Toss Brussels sprouts with 2 Tbsp. oil mixture. Place Brussels sprouts on tray in air-fryer basket; cook 4-5 minutes. Stir the sprouts. Cook until sprouts are lightly browned and near desired tenderness, about 8 minutes longer, stirring halfway through cooking time.

3. Toss bread crumbs with rosemary and remaining oil mixture; sprinkle over sprouts. Continue cooking until crumbs are browned and sprouts are tender, 3-5 minutes. Serve immediately.

¾ **cup:** 164 cal., 11g fat (1g sat. fat), 0 chol., 342mg sod., 15g carb. (3g sugars, 4g fiber), 5g pro. **Diabetic exchanges:** 2 fat, 1 vegetable, ½ starch.

CUMIN CARROTS

Carrots make a super side dish—they're big on flavor and a breeze to cook.
I can actually get my husband to eat these fragrant, deeply spiced veggies.
—Taylor Kiser, Brandon, FL

PREP: 20 MIN. • COOK: 15 MIN. • MAKES: 4 SERVINGS

2 tsp. coriander seeds
2 tsp. cumin seeds
1 lb. carrots, peeled and cut into 4x½-in. sticks
1 Tbsp. melted coconut oil or butter
2 garlic cloves, minced
¼ tsp. salt
⅛ tsp. pepper
Minced fresh cilantro, optional

1. Preheat air fryer to 325°. In a dry small skillet, toast coriander and cumin seeds over medium heat 45-60 seconds or until aromatic, stirring frequently. Cool slightly. Grind in a spice grinder, or with a mortar and pestle, until finely crushed.

2. Place carrots in a large bowl. Add melted coconut oil, garlic, salt, pepper and crushed spices; toss to coat. Place on greased tray in air-fryer basket.

3. Cook until crisp-tender and lightly browned, 12-15 minutes, stirring occasionally. If desired, sprinkle with cilantro.

1 serving: 86 cal., 4g fat (3g sat. fat), 0 chol., 228mg sod., 12g carb. (5g sugars, 4g fiber), 1g pro. **Diabetic exchanges:** 1 vegetable, 1 fat.

OKRA WITH SMOKED PAPRIKA

When you want to cook okra without frying, bake it in the air fryer with lemon juice for a lighter version. The smoked paprika gives it even more roasty oomph.
—*Lee Evans, Queen Creek, AZ*

TAKES: 20 MIN. • MAKES: 4 SERVINGS

1   lb. fresh okra pods
1   Tbsp. olive oil
1   Tbsp. lemon juice
½   tsp. smoked paprika
¼   tsp. salt
⅛   tsp. garlic powder
⅛   tsp. pepper

Preheat air fryer to 375°. Toss together all ingredients. Place okra on greased tray in air-fryer basket. Cook until tender and lightly browned, 15-20 minutes, stirring occasionally.

⅔ **cup:** 57 cal., 4g fat (1g sat. fat), 0 chol., 155mg sod., 6g carb. (3g sugars, 3g fiber), 2g pro. **Diabetic exchanges:** 1 vegetable, 1 fat.

TEST KITCHEN TIP: New to okra? It's a rich source of vitamins K and C. It's low in calories and naturally fat-free.

PARMESAN BREADED SQUASH

Yellow squash is baked to crispy perfection with this air-fyer recipe. You don't have to turn the pieces, but do keep an eye on them to be sure they don't overbrown.
—*Debi Mitchell, Flower Mound, TX*

PREP: 15 MIN. • COOK: 30 MIN./BATCH • MAKES: 4 SERVINGS

4 cups thinly sliced yellow summer squash (3 medium)
3 Tbsp. olive oil
½ tsp. salt
½ tsp. pepper
⅛ tsp. cayenne pepper
¾ cup panko bread crumbs
¾ cup grated Parmesan cheese

1. Preheat air fryer to 350°. Place squash in a large bowl. Add oil and seasonings; toss to coat.

2. In a shallow bowl, mix bread crumbs and cheese. Dip squash in crumb mixture to coat both sides, patting to help coating adhere. In batches, arrange squash in a single layer on tray in air-fryer basket. Cook until squash is tender and coating is golden brown, about 10 minutes.

½ **cup:** 203 cal., 14g fat (3g sat. fat), 11mg chol., 554mg sod., 13g carb. (4g sugars, 2g fiber), 6g pro. **Diabetic exchanges:** 3 fat, 1 vegetable, ½ starch.

ROASTED RADISHES

Radishes aren't just for salads. This abundant springtime veggie makes a colorful side dish to any meal.
—Taste of Home *Test Kitchen*

TAKES: 25 MIN. • MAKES: 6 SERVINGS

2¼ lbs. radishes, trimmed and quartered (about 6 cups)
3 Tbsp. olive oil
1 Tbsp. minced fresh oregano or 1 tsp. dried oregano
¼ tsp. salt
⅛ tsp. pepper

Preheat air fryer to 375°. Toss radishes with the remaining ingredients. Place radishes on greased tray in air-fryer basket. Cook until crisp-tender, 12-15 minutes, stirring occasionally.

⅔ **cup:** 88 cal., 7g fat (1g sat. fat), 0 chol., 165mg sod., 6g carb. (3g sugars, 3g fiber), 1g pro. **Diabetic exchanges:** 1½ fat, 1 vegetable.

TEST KITCHEN TIP: Radishes gone limp? Crisp up raw radishes by soaking them in a bowl of ice water for 5 to 10 minutes.

QUINOA ARANCINI

We love arancini, but not the fat and calories that come with them. To create a healthier version, I substituted quinoa for rice and cooked them in my air fryer. Now we can enjoy them guilt-free.

—*Sabrina Ovadia, New York, NY*

TAKES: 25 MIN. • MAKES: 3 SERVINGS

1 pkg. (9 oz.) ready-to-serve quinoa or 1¾ cups cooked quinoa
2 large eggs, lightly beaten, divided use
1 cup seasoned bread crumbs, divided
¼ cup shredded Parmesan cheese
1 Tbsp. olive oil
2 Tbsp. minced fresh basil or 2 tsp. dried basil
½ tsp. garlic powder
½ tsp. salt
⅛ tsp. pepper
6 cubes part-skim mozzarella cheese (¾ in. each)
  Cooking spray
  Warmed pasta sauce, optional

1. Preheat air fryer to 375°. Prepare quinoa according to package directions. Stir in 1 egg, ½ cup bread crumbs, Parmesan cheese, oil, basil and seasonings.

2. Divide into 6 portions. Shape each portion around a cheese cube to cover completely, forming a ball.

3. Place remaining egg and ½ cup bread crumbs in separate shallow bowls. Dip quinoa balls in egg, then roll in bread crumbs. Place on greased tray in air-fryer basket; spritz with cooking spray. Cook until golden brown, 6-8 minutes. If desired, serve with pasta sauce.

2 arancini: 423 cal., 19g fat (6g sat. fat), 142mg chol., 1283mg sod., 40g carb. (4g sugars, 5g fiber), 21g pro.

SWEET POTATOES

I can never get enough sweet potato fries! Even though my grocery store sells the bagged kind in the frozen foods section, I prefer to pull fresh spuds out of my garden and chop them up to bake in my air fryer.

—Amber Massey, Argyle, TX

TAKES: 20 MIN. • MAKES: 4 SERVINGS

2 large sweet potatoes, cut into thin strips
2 Tbsp. canola oil
1 tsp. garlic powder
1 tsp. paprika
1 tsp. kosher salt
¼ tsp. cayenne pepper

Preheat air fryer to 400°. Combine all ingredients; toss to coat. Place on greased tray in air-fryer basket. Cook until lightly browned, 10-12 minutes, stirring once. Serve immediately.

1 serving: 243 cal., 7g fat (1g sat. fat), 0 chol., 498mg sod., 43g carb. (17g sugars, 5g fiber), 3g pro.

CAULIFLOWER WITH HERBS & LEMON

A standout cauliflower side is easy to prepare with just a few ingredients.
Crushed red pepper flakes add a touch of heat.
—*Susan Hein, Burlington, WI*

TAKES: 20 MIN. • MAKES: 4 SERVINGS

1 medium head
  cauliflower, cut into
  florets (about 6 cups)
4 Tbsp. olive oil, divided
¼ cup minced fresh parsley
1 Tbsp. minced fresh
  rosemary
1 Tbsp. minced fresh thyme
1 tsp. grated lemon zest
2 Tbsp. lemon juice
½ tsp. salt
¼ tsp. crushed red
  pepper flakes

Preheat air fryer to 350°. In a large bowl, combine cauliflower and 2 Tbsp. olive, toss to coat. In batches, arrange cauliflower in a single layer on tray in air-fryer basket. Cook until florets are tender and edges are browned, 8-10 minutes, stirring halfway through. In a small bowl, combine remaining ingredients; stir in remaining 2 Tbsp. oil. Transfer cauliflower to a large bowl; drizzle with herb mixture and toss to combine.

¾ cup: 161 cal., 14g fat (2g sat. fat), 0 chol., 342mg sod., 8g carb. (3g sugars, 3g fiber), 3g pro. **Diabetic exchanges:** 3 fat, 1 vegetable.

ROASTED RED POTATOES

Fragrant rosemary, fresh or dried, gives these red potatoes a distinctive but subtle flavor. Simple to prepare, yet elegant in color and flavor, it's a wonderful addition to any menu.
—*Margie Wampler, Butler, PA*

TAKES: 20 MIN. • MAKES: 8 SERVINGS

2 lbs. small unpeeled red potatoes, cut into wedges
2 Tbsp. olive oil
1 Tbsp. minced fresh rosemary or 1 tsp. dried rosemary, crushed
2 garlic cloves, minced
½ tsp. salt
¼ tsp. pepper

1. Preheat air fryer to 400°. Drizzle potatoes with oil. Sprinkle with rosemary, garlic salt and pepper; toss gently to coat.

2. Place on ungreased tray in air-fryer basket. Cook until the potato wedges are golden brown and tender, 10-12 minutes, stirring once.

1 cup: 113 cal., 4g fat (0 sat. fat), 0 chol., 155mg sod., 18g carb. (1g sugars, 2g fiber), 2g pro. **Diabetic exchanges:** 1 starch, 1 fat.

WHY YOU'LL LOVE IT...
"What a great recipe! After reading the reviews, I decided to add some onions and mushrooms...outstanding! My husband and I devoured them and I can't wait to make this recipe again!"
—SGRONHOLZ, TASTEOFHOME.COM

CANDIED ACORN SQUASH SLICES

My grandma passed down this acorn squash recipe to me. She always served it at Thanksgiving. Now I make it whenever I'm feeling nostalgic.
—*Rita Addicks, Weimar, TX*

PREP: 15 MIN. • COOK: 15 MIN./BATCH • MAKES: 6 SERVINGS

2 medium acorn squash
⅔ cup packed brown sugar
½ cup butter, softened

1. Preheat air fryer to 350°. Cut squash in half lengthwise; remove and discard seeds. Cut each half crosswise into ½-in. slices; discard ends. In batches, arrange squash in a single layer on greased tray in air-fryer basket. Cook until just tender, 5 minutes per side.

2. Combine the sugar and butter; spread over squash. Cook 3 minutes longer.

1 serving: 320 cal., 16g fat (10g sat. fat), 41mg chol., 135mg sod., 48g carb. (29g sugars, 3g fiber), 2g pro.

EGGPLANT FRIES

Coated with Italian seasoning, Parmesan cheese and garlic salt, these veggie sticks are a favorite with my kids. I like that the eggplant is air-fried, not deep-fried, making them a smart choice for a healthy diet. Crunch away!

—Mary Murphy, Atwater, CA

PREP: 15 MIN. • COOK: 10 MIN./BATCH • MAKES: 6 SERVINGS

2 large eggs
½ cup grated Parmesan cheese
½ cup toasted wheat germ
1 tsp. Italian seasoning
¾ tsp. garlic salt
1 medium eggplant (about 1¼ lbs.)
  Cooking spray
1 cup meatless pasta sauce, warmed

1. Preheat air fryer to 375°. In a shallow bowl, whisk eggs. In another shallow bowl, mix cheese, wheat germ and seasonings.

2. Trim ends of eggplant; cut eggplant lengthwise into ½-in.-thick slices. Cut slices lengthwise into ½-in. strips. Dip eggplant in eggs, then coat with cheese mixture.

3. In batches, arrange eggplant in a single layer on greased tray in air-fryer basket; spritz slices with cooking spray. Cook until golden brown, 4-5 minutes. Turn; spritz with cooking spray. Cook until golden brown, 4-5 minutes. Serve immediately with pasta sauce.

1 serving: 135 cal., 5g fat (2g sat. fat), 68mg chol., 577mg sod., 15g carb. (6g sugars, 4g fiber), 9g pro. Diabetic Exchanges: 1 vegetable, ½ starch.

GARLIC-HERB PATTYPAN SQUASH

The first time I grew a garden, I harvested summer squash and cooked it with garlic and herbs. Using pattypan squash is a creative twist.
—Kaycee Mason, Siloam Springs, AR

TAKES: 25 MIN. • MAKES: 4 SERVINGS

5 cups halved small pattypan squash (about 1¼ lbs.)
1 Tbsp. olive oil
2 garlic cloves, minced
½ tsp. salt
¼ tsp. dried oregano
¼ tsp. dried thyme
¼ tsp. pepper
1 Tbsp. minced fresh parsley

Preheat air fryer to 375°. Place squash in a large bowl. Mix oil, garlic, salt, oregano, thyme and pepper; drizzle over squash. Toss to coat. Place squash on greased tray in air-fryer basket. Cook until tender, 10-15 minutes, stirring occasionally. Sprinkle with parsley.

⅔ **cup:** 58 cal., 3g fat (0 sat. fat), 0 chol., 296mg sod., 6g carb. (3g sugars, 2g fiber), 2g pro.

CHAPTER 4

FISH, SEAFOOD & MEATLESS

Looking to trim fat and boost your family's nutrition? Add more fresh fish and seafood to the dinner rotation, or try a meatless meal once or twice a week. Love a classic fish fry? Your catch of the day will bake up every bit as crispy and flaky when cooked in the air fryer. If you're craving a bold and tantalizing vegetarian option, see how this miracle of an appliance turns a veggie-filled dish into a meal to remember.

GENERAL TSO'S CAULIFLOWER

Cauliflower florets are deep-fried to a crispy golden brown, then coated in a sauce with just the right amount of kick. This is a fun alternative to the classic General Tso's chicken dish.

—Nick Iverson, Denver, CO

PREP: 25 MIN. • COOK: 20 MIN. • MAKES: 4 SERVINGS

½   cup all-purpose flour
½   cup cornstarch
1   tsp. salt
1   tsp. baking powder
¾   cup club soda
1   medium head cauliflower, cut into 1-in. florets (about 6 cups)

SAUCE

¼   cup orange juice
3   Tbsp. sugar
3   Tbsp. soy sauce
3   Tbsp. vegetable broth
2   Tbsp. rice vinegar
2   tsp. sesame oil
2   tsp. cornstarch
2   Tbsp. canola oil
2   to 6 dried pasilla or other hot chiles, chopped
3   green onions, white part minced, green part thinly sliced
3   garlic cloves, minced
1   tsp. grated fresh gingerroot
½   tsp. grated orange zest
4   cups hot cooked rice

1. Preheat air fryer to 400°. Combine flour, cornstarch, salt and baking powder. Stir in club soda just until blended (batter will be thin). Toss the florets in batter; transfer to a wire rack set over a baking sheet. Let stand 5 minutes. In batches, place cauliflower on greased tray in air-fryer basket. Cook until golden brown and tender, 10-12 minutes.

2. Meanwhile, whisk together first 6 sauce ingredients; whisk in cornstarch until smooth.

3. In a large saucepan, heat canola oil over medium-high heat. Add chiles; cook and stir until fragrant, 1-2 minutes. Add white part of onions, garlic, ginger and orange zest; cook until fragrant, about 1 minute. Stir orange juice mixture; add to saucepan. Bring to a boil; cook and stir until thickened, 2-4 minutes.

4. Add cauliflower to sauce; toss to coat. Serve with rice; sprinkle with thinly sliced green onions.

1 cup with 1 cup rice: 528 cal., 11g fat (1g sat. fat), 0 chol., 1614mg sod., 97g carb. (17g sugars, 5g fiber), 11g pro.

GINGERED HONEY SALMON

The ginger, garlic powder and green onion marinade give this salmon a pleasant flavor. We've found the longer it marinates, the better it tastes, especially when left overnight in the fridge We also like to use this blend when making chicken.
—*Dan Strumberger, Farmington, MN*

PREP: 10 MIN. + MARINATING • COOK: 15 MIN. • MAKES: 6 SERVINGS

⅓ cup orange juice
⅓ cup reduced-sodium soy sauce
¼ cup honey
1 green onion, chopped
1 tsp. ground ginger
1 tsp. garlic powder
1 salmon fillet (1½ lbs. and ¾ in. thick)

1. For marinade, mix the first 6 ingredients. In a shallow bowl, combine salmon and ⅔ cup marinade; refrigerate 30 minutes, turning occasionally. Reserve remaining marinade for basting.

2. Preheat air fryer to 325°. Place salmon fillet on greased tray in air-fryer basket; discard remaining marinade. Cook until fish just begins to flake easily with a fork, 15-18 minutes, basting with reserved marinade during the last 5 minutes.

3 oz. cooked fish: 237 cal., 10g fat (2g sat. fat), 57mg chol., 569mg sod., 15g carb. (13g sugars, 0 fiber), 20g pro. **Diabetic exchanges:** 3 lean meat, 1 starch.

TEST KITCHEN TIP: Ginger is available as fresh root, crystallized or ground. It has a pungent, sweet, spicy and warm notes with a slightly woody flavor.

ASIAN TOFU

This tasty Asian tofu was the first meatless recipe my fiance made for me.
It's a wonderful light protein and is so easy to pair with broiled or grilled veggies
such as eggplant, asparagus or tomatoes.

—*Emily Steers, Los Angeles, CA*

PREP: 10 MIN. + MARINATING • COOK: 10 MIN. • MAKES: 4 SERVINGS

¼ cup olive oil
3 Tbsp. reduced-sodium
   soy sauce
2 green onions, chopped
2 garlic cloves, minced
¼ tsp. ground cumin
¼ tsp. crushed red
   pepper flakes
1 pkg. (14 oz.) extra-firm tofu

1. In a bowl or shallow dish, combine the first 6 ingredients. Cut tofu lengthwise into ⅜-in. thick slices; cut each slice in half diagonally to make triangles. Add to marinade and turn to coat. Refrigerate 3-5 hours, turning occasionally.

2. Preheat air fryer to 400°. Reserving marinade, place tofu on greased tray in air-fryer basket. Drizzle remaining marinade over the tops. Cook until lightly browned and heated through, 6-8 minutes.

2 slices: 208 cal., 18g fat (3g sat. fat), 0 chol., 440mg sod., 4g carb. (1g sugars, 1g fiber), 9g pro. **Diabetic exchanges:** 3 fat, 1 lean meat.

TEST KITCHEN TIP: Tofu is also called soybean curd or bean curd. Tofu is made from soy milk, similar to the way cheese is made from dairy milk. Soy milk is mixed with calcium or magnesium salt to create curds. The more liquid (whey) is pressed from the curd, the firmer the tofu will be.

FISH & FRIES

Who doesn't love classic British pub food? These fish fillets have a fuss-free coating that's healthier but just as crunchy and golden as the deep-fried kind. Simply seasoned, the crispy fries are perfect on the side.

—Janice Mitchell, Aurora, CO

PREP: 15 MIN. • COOK: 25 MIN. • MAKES: 4 SERVINGS

1 lb. potatoes
(about 2 medium)
2 Tbsp. olive oil
¼ tsp. pepper
¼ tsp. salt

FISH
⅓ cup all-purpose flour
¼ tsp. pepper
1 large egg
2 Tbsp. water
⅔ cup crushed cornflakes
1 Tbsp. grated
Parmesan cheese
⅛ tsp. cayenne pepper
¼ tsp. salt
1 lb. haddock or cod fillets
Tartar sauce, optional

1. Preheat air fryer to 400°. Peel and cut potatoes lengthwise into ½-in.-thick slices; cut slices into ½-in.-thick sticks.

2. In a large bowl, toss potatoes with oil, pepper and salt. In batches, place potatoes in a single layer on tray in air-fryer basket; cook until just tender, 5-10 minutes Toss potatoes to redistribute; cook until lightly browned and crisp, another 5-10 minutes.

3. Meanwhile, in a shallow bowl, mix flour and pepper. In another shallow bowl, whisk egg with water. In a third bowl, toss the cornflakes with cheese and cayenne. Sprinkle fish with salt; dip into flour mixture to coat both sides; shake off excess. Dip in the egg mixture, then in cornflake mixture, patting to help coating adhere.

4. Remove fries from basket; keep warm. Place fish in a single layer on tray in air-fryer basket. Cook until fish is lightly browned and just beginning to flake easily with a fork, 8-10 minutes, turning halfway through cooking. Do not overcook. Return fries to basket to heat through. Serve immediately. If desired, serve with tartar sauce.

1 serving: 312 cal., 9g fat (2g sat. fat), 85mg chol., 503mg sod., 35g carb. (3g sugars, 1g fiber), 23g pro. **Diabetic exchanges:** 3 lean meat, 2 starch, 2 fat.

SEASONED COD

This air-fryer cod recipe will convert even the biggest fish skeptic.
It's healthy and delicious—no breading needed!
—*Kim Russell, North Wales, PA*

TAKES: 30 MIN. • MAKES: 2 SERVINGS

¼   cup fat-free Italian
     salad dressing
½   tsp. sugar
⅛   tsp. salt
⅛   tsp. garlic powder
⅛   tsp. curry powder
⅛   tsp. paprika
⅛   tsp. pepper
2   cod fillets (6 oz. each)
2   tsp. butter

1. Preheat air fryer to 370°. In a shallow bowl, mix the first 7 ingredients; add cod, turning to coat. Let stand 10-15 minutes.

2. Place fillets in a single layer on greased tray in air-fryer basket; discard remaining marinade. Cook until fish just begins to flake easily with a fork, 8-10 minutes. Top with butter.

1 fillet: 168 cal., 5g fat (3g sat. fat), 75mg chol., 366mg sod., 2g carb. (2g sugars, 0 fiber), 27g pro. **Diabetic exchanges:** 4 lean meat, 1 fat.

BREADED SCALLOPS

I never liked seafood until my husband urged me to try scallops, and now I love them. With the crunchy breading, my air-fryer scallops are the best you'll ever have.
—*Martina Preston, Willow Grove, PA*

TAKES: 25 MIN. • MAKES: 2 SERVINGS

1 large egg
⅓ cup mashed potato flakes
⅓ cup seasoned bread crumbs
⅛ tsp. salt
⅛ tsp. pepper
6 sea scallops (about ¾ lb.), patted dry
2 Tbsp. all-purpose flour
   Butter-flavored cooking spray

1. Preheat air fryer to 400°. In a shallow bowl, lightly beat egg. In another bowl, toss potato flakes, bread crumbs, salt and pepper. In a third bowl, toss scallops with flour to coat lightly. Dip in egg, then in potato mixture, patting to adhere.

2. Arrange the scallops in a single layer on greased tray in air-fryer basket; spritz with cooking spray. Cook until golden brown, 3-4 minutes. Turn; spritz with cooking spray. Cook until breading is golden brown and scallops are firm and opaque, 3-4 minutes longer.

3 scallops: 298 cal., 5g fat (1g sat. fat), 134mg chol., 1138mg sod., 33g carb. (2g sugars, 2g fiber), 28g pro.

PRETZEL-CRUSTED CATFISH

I love the flavor of this air-fried catfish. I'm not a big fish lover, so any concoction that has me loving fish is a keeper in my book. It's wonderful served with an herb rice pilaf and corn muffins with butter and honey!
—*Kelly Williams, Forked River, NJ*

PREP: 15 MIN. • COOK: 10 MIN./BATCH • MAKES: 4 SERVINGS

4 catfish fillets (6 oz. each)
½ tsp. salt
½ tsp. pepper
2 large eggs
⅓ cup Dijon mustard
2 Tbsp. 2% milk
½ cup all-purpose flour
4 cups honey mustard
   miniature pretzels,
   coarsely crushed
   Cooking spray
   Lemon slices, optional

1. Preheat air fryer to 325°. Sprinkle catfish with salt and pepper. Whisk eggs, mustard and milk in a shallow bowl. Place flour and pretzels in separate shallow bowls. Coat fillets with flour, then dip in egg mixture and coat with pretzels.

2. In batches, place the fillets in a single layer on greased tray in air-fryer basket; spritz with cooking spray. Cook until fish flakes easily with a fork, 10-12 minutes. If desired, serve with lemon slices.

1 fillet: 466 cal., 14g fat (3g sat. fat), 164mg chol., 1580mg sod., 45g carb. (2g sugars, 2g fiber), 33g pro.

SHRIMP CAESAR SALAD

My friend Jane and I have a favorite lunch spot that serves a fantastic shrimp salad. I made my own version at home so I could share it with my family and enjoy it whenever I want. To save time, buy peeled, deveined shrimp and pre-washed lettuce.
—*Marla Clark, Albuquerque, NM*

PREP: 15 MIN. • COOK: 5 MIN./BATCH • MAKES: 4 SERVINGS

2 romaine hearts, coarsely chopped
1 cup cherry tomatoes, halved
¼ cup shredded Parmesan cheese
½ cup all-purpose flour
¾ tsp. salt
½ tsp. pepper
1 lb. uncooked shrimp (26-30 per lb.), peeled and deveined
Cooking spray
½ cup creamy Caesar salad dressing

1. Preheat air fryer to 375°. In a large bowl, combine romaine, tomatoes and cheese; refrigerate until serving. In a shallow bowl, mix flour, salt and pepper. Add shrimp, a few pieces at a time, and toss to coat; shake off excess.

2. In batches, place the shrimp in a single layer on greased tray in air-fryer basket; spritz with cooking spray. Cook shrimp until lightly browned, 2-3 minutes. Turn; spritz with cooking spray. Cook until lightly browned and shrimp turn pink, 2-3 minutes longer. Remove and keep warm.

3. Drizzle dressing over romaine mixture and toss to coat. Top with shrimp. If desired, sprinkle with additional cheese and pepper; serve immediately.

1 serving: 313 cal., 21g fat (4g sat. fat), 153mg chol., 680mg sod., 8g carb. (2g sugars, 2g fiber), 23g pro.

CRUMB-TOPPED SOLE

Looking for a low-carb supper that's ready in a flash?
These buttery sole fillets are covered with a rich sauce and topped with
toasty bread crumbs. They're super speedy, thanks to your air fryer.
—Taste of Home *Test Kitchen*

PREP: 10 MIN. • COOK: 10 MIN./BATCH • MAKES: 4 SERVINGS

3   Tbsp. reduced-fat
    mayonnaise
3   Tbsp. grated Parmesan
    cheese, divided
2   tsp. mustard seed
¼   tsp. pepper
4   sole fillets (6 oz. each)
1   cup soft bread crumbs
1   green onion, finely chopped
½   tsp. ground mustard
2   tsp. butter, melted
    Cooking spray

1. Preheat air fryer to 375°. Combine mayonnaise, 2 Tbsp. cheese, mustard seed and pepper; spread over tops of fillets.

2. Place fish in a single layer on greased tray in air-fryer basket. Cook until fish flakes easily with a fork, 3-5 minutes.

3. Meanwhile, in a small bowl, combine bread crumbs, onion, ground mustard and remaining 1 Tbsp. cheese; stir in butter. Spoon over fillets, patting gently to adhere; spritz topping with cooking spray. Cook until golden brown, 2-3 minutes longer. If desired, sprinkle with additional green onions.

1 fillet: 233 cal., 11g fat (3g sat. fat), 89mg chol., 714mg sod., 8g carb. (1g sugars, 1g fiber), 24g pro.

SALSA BLACK BEAN BURGERS

Your family will look forward to meatless meals when these hearty bean burgers are on the menu. Guacamole and sour cream make them extra delicious.
—*Jill Reichardt, St. Louis, MO*

TAKES: 30 MIN. • MAKES: 4 SERVINGS

1 can (15 oz.) black beans, rinsed and drained
⅔ cup dry bread crumbs
1 small tomato, seeded and finely chopped
1 jalapeno pepper, seeded and finely chopped
1 large egg
1 tsp. minced fresh cilantro
1 garlic clove, minced
1 Tbsp. olive oil
4 whole wheat hamburger buns, split
Reduced-fat sour cream and guacamole, optional

1. Preheat air fryer to 375°. Place beans in a food processor; cover and process until blended. Transfer to a large bowl. Add bread crumbs, tomato, jalapeno, egg, cilantro and garlic. Mix until combined. Shape into 4 patties.

2. In batches, place patties on greased tray in air-fryer basket. Cook until lightly browned, 3-4 minutes. Turn; cook until lightly browned, 3-4 minutes longer. Serve on buns. If desired, top with sour cream and guacamole.

1 burger: 323 cal., 8g fat (1g sat. fat), 47mg chol., 576mg sod., 51g carb. (6g sugars, 9g fiber), 13g pro.

TEST KITCHEN TIP: Always rinse and drain canned beans before using to reduce sodium content and gas-producing sugars.

COCONUT SHRIMP & APRICOT SAUCE

Shredded coconut and panko crumbs give these spicy air-fryer shrimp a delectable crunch. Enjoy them as an appetizer or serve with hush puppies and rye bread for a complete meal.
—*Debi Mitchell, Flower Mound, TX*

PREP: 25 MIN. • COOK: 10 MIN./BATCH • MAKES: 6 SERVINGS

1½ lbs. uncooked large shrimp
1½ cups sweetened shredded coconut
½ cup panko bread crumbs
4 large egg whites
3 dashes Louisiana-style hot sauce
¼ tsp. salt
¼ tsp. pepper
½ cup all-purpose flour

SAUCE
1 cup apricot preserves
1 tsp. cider vinegar
¼ tsp. crushed red pepper flakes

1. Preheat air fryer to 375°. Peel and devein the shrimp, leaving tails on.

2. In a shallow bowl, toss coconut with bread crumbs. In another shallow bowl, whisk the egg whites, hot sauce, salt and pepper. Place flour in a third shallow bowl.

3. Dip shrimp in flour to coat lightly; shake off excess. Dip in egg white mixture, then in coconut mixture, patting to help coating adhere.

4. In batches, place shrimp in a single layer on greased tray in air-fryer basket. Cook 4 minutes. Turn shrimp; cook until coconut is lightly browned and shrimp turn pink, about 4 minutes longer.

5. Meanwhile, combine sauce ingredients in a small saucepan; cook and stir over medium-low heat until preserves are melted. Serve shrimp immediately with sauce.

6 shrimp with 2 Tbsp. sauce: 410 cal., 10g fat (8g sat. fat), 138mg chol., 418mg sod., 58g carb. (34g sugars, 2g fiber), 24g pro.

CHAPTER 5

PORK

Go ahead and pig out! Everyone's granted permission to dig in when pork is on the menu. Smart cooks reach for this budget-friendly and versatile meat for a variety of mealtime solutions, and making it in the air fryer makes it even easier and more delicious. With everything from tender shredded pork, finger-licking chops, petite medallions and more, these meaty favorites cook up fast and are guaranteed to satisfy the heartiest of appetites.

LOADED PORK BURRITOS

Burritos are the perfect dinner for the whole family, especially this quick and easy recipe. Don't be afraid to load yours up with pork, beans, cheese and rice.
—Fiona Seels, Pittsburgh, PA

PREP: 35 MIN. + MARINATING • COOK: 5 MIN. • MAKES: 6 SERVINGS

¾ cup thawed limeade concentrate
1 Tbsp. olive oil
2 tsp. salt, divided
1½ tsp. pepper, divided
1½ lbs. boneless pork loin, cut into thin strips
1 cup chopped seeded plum tomatoes
1 small green pepper, chopped
1 small onion, chopped
¼ cup plus ⅓ cup minced fresh cilantro, divided
1 jalapeno pepper, seeded and chopped
1 Tbsp. lime juice
¼ tsp. garlic powder
1 cup uncooked long grain rice
3 cups shredded Monterey Jack cheese
6 flour tortillas (12 in.), warmed
1 can (15 oz.) black beans, rinsed and drained
1½ cups sour cream
Cooking spray

1. In a large shallow dish, combine the limeade concentrate, oil, 1 tsp. salt and ½ tsp. pepper; add pork. Turn to coat; cover and refrigerate at least 20 minutes.

2. For salsa, in a small bowl, combine the tomatoes, green pepper, onion, ¼ cup cilantro, jalapeno, lime juice, garlic powder and remaining salt and pepper. Set aside.

3. Meanwhile, cook rice according to package directions. Stir in remaining cilantro; keep warm.

4. Drain pork, discarding marinade. Preheat air fryer to 350°. In batches, place pork in a single layer on greased tray in air-fryer basket; spritz with cooking spray. Cook until pork is no longer pink, 8-10 minutes, turning halfway through.

5. Sprinkle ⅓ cup cheese off-center on each tortilla. Layer each with ¼ cup salsa, ½ cup rice mixture, ¼ cup black beans and ¼ cup sour cream, top with about ½ cup pork. Fold sides and ends over filling. Serve with remaining salsa.

1 burrito: 910 cal., 42g fat (22g sat. fat), 119mg chol., 1768mg sod., 82g carb. (11g sugars, 9g fiber), 50g pro.

RASPBERRY BALSAMIC SMOKED PORK CHOPS

Air fryer pork chops are so delicious and so easy to make. My husband loves them.
—*Lynn Moretti, Oconomowoc, WI*

PREP: 15 MIN. • COOK: 15 MIN./BATCH • MAKES: 4 SERVINGS

2 large eggs
¼ cup 2% milk
1 cup panko bread crumbs
1 cup finely chopped pecans
4 smoked bone-in pork chops (7½ oz. each)
¼ cup all-purpose flour
  Cooking spray
⅓ cup balsamic vinegar
2 Tbsp. brown sugar
2 Tbsp. seedless raspberry jam
1 Tbsp. thawed frozen orange juice concentrate

1. Preheat air fryer to 400°. In a shallow bowl, whisk together eggs and milk. In another shallow bowl, toss bread crumbs with pecans.

2. Coat pork chops with flour; shake off excess. Dip in the egg mixture, then in the crumb mixture, patting to help adhere. In batches, place chops in single layer on greased tray in air-fryer basket; spritz with cooking spray.

3. Cook until golden brown and a thermometer inserted in pork reads 145°, 12-15 minutes, turning halfway through cooking and spritzing with additional cooking spray. Meanwhile, place remaining ingredients in a small saucepan; bring to a boil. Cook and stir until slightly thickened, 6-8 minutes. Serve with chops.

1 pork chop with 1 Tbsp. glaze: 579 cal., 36g fat (10g sat. fat), 106mg chol., 1374mg sod., 36g carb. (22g sugars, 3g fiber), 32g pro.

LOW-CARB PORK CHOPS

These pork chops get their bold flavor from Creole seasoning and Parmesan cheese. Bonus: They're low in carbs, too! The recipe is definitely a keeper in my book.
—*Dawn Parker, Surrey, BC*

PREP: 25 MIN. MAKES: 4 SERVINGS

4 boneless pork loin chops (6 oz. each)
⅓ cup almond flour
¼ cup grated Parmesan cheese
1 teaspoon garlic powder
1 teaspoon Creole seasoning
1 teaspoon paprika
Cooking spray

1. Preheat air fryer to 375°. Spritz fryer basket with cooking spray. In a shallow bowl, toss almond flour, cheese, garlic powder, Creole seasoning and paprika. Coat pork chops with flour mixture; shake off excess. Working in batches as needed, place the chops in single layer in air-fryer basket; spritz with cooking spray.

2. Cook until golden brown, 12-15 minutes or until a thermometer reads 145°, turning halfway through cooking and spritzing with additional cooking spray. Remove and keep warm. Repeat with remaining chops.

1 pork chop: 310 cal., 16g fat (5g sat. fat), 86mg chol., 308mg sod., 4g carb. (0 sugars, 1g fiber), 36g pro. **Diabetic exchanges:** 5 lean meat, 2 fat.

JAMAICAN JERK PORK CHOPS

These sweet, spicy chops come together in minutes, but you'd never guess
it from how good they taste. Serve them with a side of jasmine rice and you'll feel
like you're on a tropical vacation.
—*Allison Ulrich, Frisco, TX*

TAKES: 25 MIN. • MAKES: 2 SERVINGS

1   Tbsp. butter, softened
¼   cup peach preserves
4   boneless thin-cut pork loin
    chops (2 to 3 oz. each)
3   tsp. Caribbean jerk
    seasoning
½   tsp. salt
¼   tsp. pepper
½   medium sweet
    orange pepper
½   medium sweet
    yellow pepper
½   medium sweet red pepper
    Hot cooked rice, optional

1. Preheat air fryer to 350°. In a small bowl, mix butter and peach preserves until combined; set aside.

2. Sprinkle the chops with seasonings. Place on greased tray in air-fryer basket. Cook until no longer pink, 2-3 minutes on each side. Remove and keep warm.

3. Cut peppers into thin strips. Place on greased tray in air-fryer basket. Cook until crisp-tender and lightly browned, 5-6 minutes, stirring occasionally. Return chops to air fryer; top with butter mixture. Cook until the butter is melted, 1-2 minutes. If desired, serve with rice.

1 serving: 368 cal., 14g fat (7g sat. fat), 84mg chol., 1099mg sod., 32g carb. (28g sugars, 2g fiber), 28g pro.

PORK SCHNITZEL

This recipe is one of my husband's favorites because it reminds him of his German roots. Cooking pork schnitzel in an air fryer is genius because we can eat in a jiffy.

—Joyce Folker, Parowan, UT

PREP: 20 MIN. • COOK: 10 MIN. • MAKES: 4 SERVINGS

¼ cup all-purpose flour
1 tsp. seasoned salt
¼ tsp. pepper
1 large egg
2 Tbsp. 2% milk
¾ cup dry bread crumbs
1 tsp. paprika
4 pork sirloin cutlets
 (4 oz. each)
 Cooking spray

DILL SAUCE
1 Tbsp. all-purpose flour
¾ cup chicken broth
½ cup sour cream
¼ tsp. dill weed

1. Preheat air fryer to 375°. In a shallow bowl, mix the flour, seasoned salt and pepper. In a second shallow bowl, whisk egg and milk until blended. In a third bowl, mix bread crumbs and paprika.

2. Pound pork cutlets with a meat mallet to ¼-in. thickness. Dip cutlets in flour mixture to coat both sides; shake off excess. Dip in egg mixture, then in crumb mixture, patting to help coating adhere to the pork.

3. Place the pork in a single layer on greased tray in air-fryer basket; spritz with cooking spray. Cook until golden brown, 4-5 minutes. Turn; spritz with cooking spray. Cook until golden brown, 4-5 minutes longer. Remove to a serving plate; keep warm.

4. Meanwhile, in a small saucepan, whisk flour and broth until smooth. Bring to a boil, stirring constantly; cook and stir for 2 minutes or until thickened. Reduce heat to low. Stir in sour cream and dill; heat through (do not boil). Serve with pork.

1 serving: 309 cal., 13g fat (5g sat. fat), 91mg chol., 572mg sod., 17g carb. (2g sugars, 1g fiber), 30g pro.

GREEN TOMATO STACKS

This recipe is for tomato lovers. When I ran across the recipe, I had to try it. A slice of Canadian bacon and a citrus-infused sauce take it to another level.
—*Barbara Mohr, Millington, MI*

PREP: 20 MIN. • COOK: 15 MIN./BATCH • MAKES: 8 SERVINGS

¼ cup fat-free mayonnaise
¼ tsp. grated lime zest
2 Tbsp. lime juice
1 tsp. minced fresh thyme
   or ¼ tsp. dried thyme
½ tsp. pepper, divided
¼ cup all-purpose flour
2 large egg whites,
   lightly beaten
¾ cup cornmeal
¼ tsp. salt
2 medium green tomatoes
2 medium red tomatoes
   Cooking spray
8 slices Canadian
   bacon, warmed

1. Preheat air fryer to 375°. Mix mayonnaise, lime zest and juice, thyme and ¼ tsp. pepper; refrigerate until serving. Place flour in a shallow bowl; place egg whites in a separate shallow bowl. In a third bowl, mix cornmeal, salt and remaining ¼ tsp. pepper.

2. Cut each tomato crosswise into 4 slices. Lightly coat each slice in flour; shake off excess. Dip in egg whites, then in cornmeal mixture.

3. In batches, place tomatoes on greased tray in air-fryer basket; spritz with cooking spray. Cook until golden brown, 4-6 minutes. Turn; spritz with cooking spray. Cook until golden brown, 4-6 minutes longer.

4. For each serving, stack 1 slice each green tomato, bacon and red tomato. Serve with sauce.

1 stack: 114 cal., 2g fat (0 sat. fat), 7mg chol., 338mg sod., 18g carb. (3g sugars, 2g fiber), 6g pro. **Diabetic exchanges:** 1 starch, 1 lean meat, 1 vegetable.

STUFFED PORK CHOPS

Don't wait for Thanksgiving to enjoy homemade stuffing. These pork chops are one of my favorite dishes to serve guests. A sure hit, they can be enjoyed any time of year and are a nice variation from turkey.
—*Lorraine Darocha, Mountain City, TN*

PREP: 40 MIN. • COOK: 20 MIN. • MAKES: 4 SERVINGS

½ tsp. olive oil
1 celery rib, chopped
¼ cup chopped onion
4 slices white bread, cubed
2 Tbsp. minced fresh parsley
⅛ tsp. salt
⅛ tsp. rubbed sage
⅛ tsp. white pepper
⅛ tsp. dried marjoram
⅛ tsp. dried thyme
⅓ cup reduced-sodium chicken broth

PORK CHOPS
4 pork rib chops (7 oz. each)
¼ tsp. salt
¼ tsp. pepper

1. In a large skillet, heat oil over medium-high heat. Add celery and onion; cook and stir until tender, 4-5 minutes. Remove from the heat. In a large bowl, combine bread and seasonings. Add celery mixture and broth; toss to coat. Set aside.

2. Cut a pocket in each pork chop by making a horizontal slice almost to the bone. Fill chops with bread mixture; secure with toothpicks if necessary.

3. Preheat air-fryer to 325°. Sprinkle chops with salt and pepper. Arrange in single layer on greased tray in air-fryer basket. Cook 10 minutes. Turn and cook until a thermometer inserted into center of stuffing reads 165° and thermometer inserted in pork reads at least 145°, 6-8 minutes longer. Let stand 5 minutes; discard toothpicks before serving.

1 pork chop: 274 cal., 10g fat (4g sat. fat), 63mg chol., 457mg sod., 16g carb. (2g sugars, 1g fiber), 28g pro. **Diabetic exchanges:** 4 lean meat, 1 starch.

TEST KITCHEN TIP: There are different types of pork chops. A pork loin chop has a T-bone-shaped bone, with meat on both sides of the bone. A rib chop has meat nestled between the rib and backbone. Center cut chops are boneless. A blade chop may have bones from the shoulder blade, rib and back.

SWEET & SOUR PORK

Whether you're serving a party of two or making a bigger batch
for company, you'll find this succulent pork tenderloin a top choice.
—*Leigh Rys, Herndon, VA*

PREP: 25 MIN. • COOK: 15 MIN. • MAKES: 2 SERVINGS

½ cup unsweetened crushed
   pineapple, undrained
½ cup cider vinegar
¼ cup sugar
¼ cup packed dark
   brown sugar
¼ cup ketchup
1 Tbsp. reduced-sodium
   soy sauce
1½ tsp. Dijon mustard
½ tsp. garlic powder
1 pork tenderloin
   (¾ lb.), halved
⅛ tsp. salt
⅛ tsp. pepper
   Sliced green onions,
   optional
   Cooking spray

1. In a small saucepan, combine the first 8 ingredients. Bring to a boil; reduce the heat. Simmer, uncovered, until thickened, 6-8 minutes, stirring occasionally.

2. Preheat air fryer to 350°. Sprinkle pork with salt and pepper. Place the pork on greased tray in air-fryer basket; spritz with cooking spray. Cook until pork begins to brown around edges, 7-8 minutes. Turn; pour 2 Tbsp. sauce over pork. Cook until a thermometer inserted into the pork reads at least 145°, 10-12 minutes longer. Let stand 5 minutes before slicing. Serve with remaining sauce. If desired, top with sliced green onions.

5 oz. cooked pork with ½ cup sauce: 502 cal., 7g fat (2g sat. fat), 95mg chol., 985mg sod., 72g carb. (69g sugars, 1g fiber), 35g pro.

TEST KITCHEN TIP: Since this recipe calls for only 1 Tbsp. soy sauce, you can use soy sauce packets from your local Chinese restaurant instead of buying a bottle. Use reduced-sodium, if available, to reduce the sodium content. To cut even more, replace some of the soy sauce with reduced-sodium broth or water.

JAPANESE TONKATSU

I have my dear friend Junie Obi to thank for my love of tonkatsu. Her mom owned a food stand that served these traditional Japanese breaded pork cutlets. She shared the recipe with me years ago, and it continues to be a favorite.
—*Yuko Shibata, Monterey Park, CA*

PREP: 20 MIN. • COOK: 5 MIN./BATCH • MAKES: 4 SERVINGS

4   boneless pork loin
    chops (6 oz. each)
3   Tbsp. all-purpose flour
1   Tbsp. garlic salt
2   large eggs
2   cups panko bread crumbs
    Butter-flavored cooking
    spray

SAUCE
¼   cup ketchup
2   Tbsp. Worcestershire sauce
1   Tbsp. sugar
1   Tbsp. reduced-sodium
    soy sauce
2   tsp. prepared hot mustard

1. Preheat air fryer to 375°. Flatten the pork chops to ¼-in. thickness. In a shallow bowl, combine flour and garlic salt. In a separate shallow bowl, whisk eggs. Place bread crumbs in a third bowl. Coat pork with flour mixture, then dip in eggs and coat in crumbs.

2. In batches, place pork chops in a single layer on greased tray in air-fryer basket; spritz with cooking spray. Cook until crisp, 5 minutes. Turn; spritz with cooking spray. Cook until crisp and juices run clear, 5-6 minutes longer.

3. Meanwhile, in a small bowl, combine the sauce ingredients; serve with pork.

1 serving: 391 cal., 14g fat (4g sat. fat), 175mg chol., 1320mg sod., 25g carb. (9g sugars, 1g fiber), 39g pro.

CHICKEN CORDON BLEU

One of my son's favorite ways to eat chicken is when it's wrapped with ham and Swiss cheese. My recipe has all the yummy flavors of the classic dish in a 30-minute meal, and leftovers freeze well.
—*Ronda Eagle, Goose Creek, SC*

TAKES: 30 MIN. • MAKES: 4 SERVINGS

4 boneless skinless chicken breast halves (4 oz. each)
¼ tsp. salt
¼ tsp. pepper
4 slices deli ham
2 slices aged Swiss cheese, halved
1 cup panko bread crumbs
Cooking spray

SAUCE
1 Tbsp. all-purpose flour
½ cup 2% milk
¼ cup dry white wine
3 Tbsp. finely shredded Swiss cheese
⅛ tsp. salt
Dash pepper

1. Preheat air fryer to 365°. Sprinkle chicken breasts with salt and pepper. Place on greased tray in air-fryer basket. Cook 10 minutes. Top each with 1 slice ham and a ½ slice cheese, folding ham in half and covering chicken as much as possible. Sprinkle with the bread crumbs. Carefully spritz crumbs with cooking spray. Cook until a thermometer inserted in chicken reads 165°, 5-7 minutes longer.

2. For sauce, in a small saucepan, whisk flour and milk until smooth. Bring to a boil, stirring constantly; cook and stir for 1-2 minutes or until thickened.

3. Reduce to medium heat. Stir in wine and cheese; cook and stir 2-3 minutes or until cheese is melted and sauce is thickened and bubbly. Stir in salt and pepper. Keep warm over low heat until ready to serve. Serve with chicken.

1 chicken breast half with 3 Tbsp. sauce: 272 cal., 8g fat (3g sat. fat), 83mg chol., 519mg sod., 14g carb. (2g sugars, 1g fiber), 32g pro. **Diabetic exchanges:** 4 lean meat, 1 starch, 1 fat.

APRICOT-ROSEMARY PORK MEDALLIONS

I had a pork tenderloin in my fridge that I needed to use before it expired, but I didn't want to wait for it to roast in the oven. I tried the air-fryer method, and not only was it quick, but my family loved it. Try different preserves to make your favorite flavors.
—Lynn Caruso, Gilroy, CA

PREP: 10 MIN. • COOK: 30 MIN. • MAKES: 4 SERVINGS

1 pork tenderloin (1 lb.)
¼ cup seasoned bread crumbs
Cooking spray
3 cups fresh broccoli florets
⅓ cup apricot preserves
2 Tbsp. white wine or chicken broth
1 tsp. minced fresh rosemary or ¼ tsp. dried rosemary, crushed
¼ tsp. salt
Dash pepper
2⅔ cups hot cooked brown rice

1. Preheat air fryer to 375°. Cut pork tenderloin crosswise into 8 slices. Place bread crumbs in a shallow bowl. Dip pork slices in crumbs, patting to help coating adhere. In batches, place pork on greased tray in air-fryer basket; spritz with cooking spray. Cook until a thermometer reads 145°, 4-5 minutes per side. Remove and keep warm.

2. Place broccoli on tray in air-fryer basket. Cook until tender, 4-6 minutes, stirring once.

3. In a small saucepan, mix preserves, wine, rosemary, salt and pepper. Cook and stir over medium-low heat until preserves are melted, 3-5 minutes. Serve with pork, broccoli and rice.

1 serving: 405 cal., 6g fat (2g sat. fat), 64mg chol., 289mg sod., 58g carb. (13g sugars, 4g fiber), 29g pro.

TEST KITCHEN TIP: Rosemary is available dried or as fresh leaves on stems. It has a pungent flavor with a hint of pine. It is commonly used to flavor pork, lamb, poultry and vegetables.

CHAPTER 6

POULTRY

What's for supper tonight? For a family-friendly dish that's both comforting and hearty, chicken is your best bet. But no need to heat up the oven because these air-fryer recipes are guaranteed to be new favorites. Coat chicken in breadcrumbs to create a healthier alternative to fried chicken, or cook it without breading to enjoy the most flavorful, tender chicken of your life.

BREADED CHICKEN TENDERS

I took all of the components of a loaded baked potato—cheddar, potato, bacon, sour cream and chives—and turned it into my latest quick and easy dish. Every kid will love these air-fryer chicken tenders!
—*Cyndy Gerken, Naples, FL*

PREP: 25 MIN. • COOK: 15 MIN./BATCH • MAKES: 4 SERVINGS

½ cup panko bread crumbs
½ cup potato sticks, crushed
½ cup crushed cheese crackers
¼ cup grated Parmesan cheese
2 bacon strips, cooked and crumbled
2 tsp. minced fresh chives
¼ cup butter, melted
1 Tbsp. sour cream
1 lb. chicken tenderloins

1. Preheat air fryer to 400°. In a shallow bowl, combine the first 6 ingredients. In another shallow bowl, whisk butter and sour cream. Dip chicken in butter mixture, then in crumb mixture, patting to help coating adhere.

2. In batches, arrange chicken in a single layer on greased tray in air-fryer basket; spritz with cooking spray. Cook until coating is golden brown and chicken is no longer pink, 7-8 minutes on each side. Serve with additional sour cream and chives.

1 serving: 256 cal., 14g fat (7g sat. fat), 84mg chol., 267mg sod., 6g carb. (0 sugars, 0 fiber), 29g pro.

SOUTHERN-STYLE CHICKEN

I call this America's best-loved air-fryer chicken. The secret is in the breading, which makes the chicken super moist and flavorful, herby and golden brown.
—*Elaina Morgan, Rickman, TN*

PREP:15 MIN. • COOK: 20 MIN./BATCH • MAKES: 6 SERVINGS

2 cups crushed Ritz crackers (about 50)
1 Tbsp. minced fresh parsley
1 tsp. garlic salt
1 tsp. paprika
½ tsp. pepper
¼ tsp. ground cumin
¼ tsp. rubbed sage
1 large egg, beaten
1 broiler/fryer chicken (3 to 4 lbs.), cut up
   Cooking spray

1. Preheat the air fryer to 375°. In a shallow bowl, mix the first 7 ingredients. Place egg in a separate shallow bowl. Dip chicken in egg, then in cracker mixture, patting to help coating adhere. In batches, place chicken in a single layer on greased tray in air-fryer basket, spritz with cooking spray.

2. Cook 10 minutes. Turn chicken pieces and spritz with cooking spray; cook until chicken is golden brown and juices run clear, 10-20 minutes longer.

5 oz. cooked chicken: 410 cal., 23g fat (6g sat. fat), 135mg chol., 460mg sod., 13g carb. (2g sugars, 1g fiber), 36g pro.

THAI CHICKEN MEATBALLS

These Thai chicken meatballs make a great game-day snack.
We also like to serve them as a main dish over stir-fried veggies.
—*Merry Graham, Newhall, CA*

PREP: 10 MIN. • COOK: 10 MIN./BATCH • MAKES: 12 SERVINGS

½ cup sweet chili sauce
2 Tbsp. lime juice
2 Tbsp. ketchup
1 tsp. soy sauce
1 large egg, lightly beaten
¾ cup panko bread crumbs
1 green onion, finely chopped
1 Tbsp. minced fresh cilantro
½ tsp. salt
½ tsp. garlic powder
1 lb. lean ground chicken

1. Preheat air fryer to 350°. In a small bowl, combine chili sauce, lime juice, ketchup and soy sauce; reserve ½ cup for serving. In a large bowl, combine egg, bread crumbs, green onion, cilantro, salt, garlic powder and remaining 4 Tbsp. chili sauce mixture. Add chicken; mix lightly but thoroughly. Shape into 12 balls.

2. In batches, arrange meatballs in a single layer on greased tray in air-fryer basket. Cook until lightly browned, 4-5 minutes. Turn and cook until lightly browned and cooked through, 4-5 minutes longer. Serve meatballs with reserved sauce, sprinkling with additional cilantro if desired.

1 meatball: 98 cal., 3g fat (1g sat. fat), 43mg chol., 369mg sod., 9g carb. (6g sugars, 0 fiber), 9g pro.

TEST KITCHEN TIP: Cilantro is available as fresh or dried leaves. It has a pungent, strong flavor from same plant as coriander seeds. For some, it strongly resembles the taste of soap. Feel free to reduce or omit the herb in this recipe to suit your tastes.

EVERYTHING BAGEL CHICKEN STRIPS

I love the flavor profile of everything bagels, so I recreated it with traditional breaded chicken fingers. Serve them with your favorite dipping sauce.
—*Cyndy Gerken, Naples, FL*

PREP: 10 MIN. • COOK: 15 MIN./BATCH • MAKES: 4 SERVINGS

1 day-old everything bagel, torn
½ cup panko bread crumbs
½ cup grated Parmesan cheese
¼ tsp. crushed red pepper flakes
¼ cup butter, cubed
1 lb. chicken tenderloins
½ tsp. salt

1. Preheat air fryer to 400°. Pulse the bagel pieces in a food processor until coarse crumbs form. Place ½ cup bagel crumbs in a shallow bowl; toss with panko, cheese and pepper flakes. (Discard or save remaining bagel crumbs for another use.)

2. In a microwave-safe shallow bowl, microwave butter until melted. Sprinkle chicken with salt. Dip in warm butter, then coat with crumb mixture, patting to help adhere. In batches, place chicken in a single layer on greased tray in air-fryer basket.

3. Cook 7 minutes; turn chicken. Continue cooking until coating is golden brown and chicken is no longer pink, 7-8 minutes. Serve immediately.

1 serving: 269 cal., 13g fat (7g sat. fat), 88mg chol., 663mg sod., 8g carb. (1g sugars, 0 fiber), 31g pro.

CRISPY CURRY DRUMSTICKS

These air-fryer chicken drumsticks are flavorful, crispy on the outside and juicy on the inside. Sometimes I'll add some red pepper flakes in addition to the curry powder if I want to spice it up a bit. I like to serve it with chicken-seasoned rice and boiled broccoli.
—*Zena Furgason, Norman, OK*

PREP: 35 MIN. • COOK: 15 MIN./BATCH • MAKES: 4 SERVINGS

1 lb. chicken drumsticks
¾ tsp. salt, divided
2 Tbsp. olive oil
2 tsp. curry powder
½ tsp. onion salt
½ tsp. garlic powder
   Minced fresh cilantro,
   optional

1. In a large bowl, place chicken and enough water to cover. Add ½ tsp. salt; let stand 15 minutes at room temperature. Drain and pat dry.

2. Preheat air fryer to 375°. In a another bowl, mix the oil, curry powder, onion salt, garlic powder and remaining ¼ tsp. salt; add chicken and toss to coat. In batches, place chicken in a single layer on tray in air-fryer basket. Cook until a thermometer inserted in chicken reads 170°-175°, 15-17 minutes, turning halfway through. If desired, sprinkle with cilantro.

2 oz. cooked chicken: 180 cal., 13g fat (3g sat. fat), 47mg chol., 711mg sod., 1g carb. (0 sugars, 1g fiber), 15g pro.

TURKEY CLUB ROULADES

Weeknights turn elegant when these short-prep roulades with familiar ingredients are on the menu. Not a fan of turkey? Substitute lightly pounded chicken breasts.
—Taste of Home *Test Kitchen*

PREP: 20 MIN. • COOK: 10 MIN./BATCH • MAKES: 8 SERVINGS

¾ lb. fresh asparagus, trimmed
8 turkey breast cutlets (about 1 lb.)
1 Tbsp. Dijon-mayonnaise blend
8 slices deli ham
8 slices provolone cheese
½ tsp. poultry seasoning
½ tsp. pepper
8 bacon strips

SAUCE
⅔ cup Dijon-mayonnaise blend
4 tsp. 2% milk
¼ tsp. poultry seasoning

1. Preheat air fryer to 375°. Place asparagus on greased tray in air-fryer basket. Cook until crisp-tender, 4-5 minutes, tossing halfway through cooking. Set aside.

2. Spread turkey cutlets with Dijon-mayonnaise. Layer with ham, cheese and asparagus. Sprinkle with poultry seasoning and pepper. Roll up tightly and wrap with bacon.

3. In batches, arrange roulades in a single layer on greased tray in air-fryer basket. Cook until bacon is crisp and turkey is no longer pink, 8-10 minutes, turning occasionally. Combine sauce ingredients; serve with roulades.

1 roulade with 1 Tbsp. sauce: 224 cal., 11g fat (5g sat. fat), 64mg chol., 1075mg sod., 2g carb. (1g sugars, 0 fiber), 25g pro.

WHY YOU'LL LOVE IT...
"These were amazing. I followed the recipe except that I roasted my asparagus first. Very delicious. These will be on my menu more frequently."
—PAJAMAANGEL, TASTEOFHOME.COM

SWEET POTATO-CRUSTED CHICKEN NUGGETS

I was looking for creative ways to spice up traditional chicken nuggets and came up with this recipe. The sweet potato chips add a crunchy texture and flavor on the outside, while the meat stays tender on the inside.
—*Kristina Segarra, Yonkers, NY*

PREP: 15 MIN. • COOK: 10 MIN./BATCH • MAKES: 4 SERVINGS

1 cup sweet potato chips
¼ cup all-purpose flour
1 tsp. salt, divided
½ tsp. coarsely ground pepper
¼ tsp. baking powder
1 Tbsp. cornstarch
1 lb. chicken tenderloins, cut into 1½-in. pieces
Cooking spray

1. Preheat air fryer to 400°. Place chips, flour, ½ tsp. salt, pepper and baking powder in a food processor; pulse until ground. Transfer to a shallow dish.

2. Mix cornstarch and remaining ½ tsp. salt; toss with chicken. Toss chicken with potato chip mixture, pressing to coat.

3. In batches, arrange chicken in a single layer on greased tray in air-fryer basket; spritz with cooking spray. Cook until golden brown, 3-4 minutes. Turn; spritz with cooking spray. Cook until golden brown and chicken is no longer pink, 3-4 minutes longer.

3 oz. cooked chicken: 190 cal., 4g fat (0 sat. fat), 56mg chol., 690mg sod., 13g carb. (1g sugars, 1g fiber), 28g pro. **Diabetic exchanges:** 3 lean meat, 1 starch.

TURKEY CROQUETTES

I grew up with a family that looked forward to leftovers, especially the day after Thanksgiving. But we didn't just reheat turkey and spuds in the microwave—we took our culinary creativity to a new level with recipes likes these croquettes. Serve three per plate along with a crisp green salad for an unforgettable meal.
—*Meredith Coe, Charlottesville, VA*

PREP: 20 MIN. • COOK: 10 MIN./BATCH • MAKES: 6 SERVINGS

2 cups mashed potatoes (with added milk and butter)
½ cup grated Parmesan cheese
½ cup shredded Swiss cheese
1 shallot, finely chopped
2 tsp. minced fresh rosemary or ½ tsp. dried rosemary, crushed
1 tsp. minced fresh sage or ¼ tsp. dried sage leaves
½ tsp. salt
¼ tsp. pepper
3 cups finely chopped cooked turkey
1 large egg
2 Tbsp. water
1¼ cups panko bread crumbs
Butter-flavored cooking spray
Sour cream, optional

1. Preheat air fryer to 350°. In a large bowl, combine mashed potatoes, cheeses, shallot, rosemary, sage, salt and pepper; stir in turkey. Shape into twelve 1-in.-thick patties.

2. In a shallow bowl, whisk egg and water. Place bread crumbs in another shallow bowl. Dip croquettes in egg mixture, then in bread crumbs, patting to help coating adhere.

3. In batches, place croquettes in a single layer on greased tray in air-fryer basket; spritz with cooking spray. Cook until golden brown, 4-5 minutes. Turn; spritz with cooking spray. Cook until golden brown; 4-5 minutes. If desired, serve with sour cream.

2 croquettes: 322 cal., 12g fat (6g sat. fat), 124mg chol., 673mg sod., 22g carb. (2g sugars, 2g fiber), 29g pro. **Diabetic exchanges:** 4 lean meat, 1½ starch, 1 fat.

ALMOND CHICKEN

My husband bought an air fryer a few months ago, after seeing a promotion on television. Since then, we have used it at least twice a week and love how delicious the food turns out. The chicken recipes we have tried are especially good because how moist the meat remains. We started a low-carb diet and did not want to use bread crumbs so we tried the chicken with almonds. It's a favorite now.
—*Pamela Shank, Parkersburg, WV*

TAKES: 30 MIN. • MAKES: 2 SERVINGS

1   large egg
¼   cup buttermilk
1   tsp. garlic salt
½   tsp. pepper
1   cup slivered almonds, finely chopped
2   boneless skinless chicken breast halves (6 oz. each)
    Optional: Ranch salad dressing, barbecue sauce or honey mustard

1. Preheat air fryer to 350°. In a shallow bowl, whisk egg, buttermilk, garlic salt and pepper. Place almonds in another shallow bowl. Dip chicken in egg mixture, then in almonds, patting to help coating adhere.

2. Place chicken in a single layer on greased tray in air-fryer basket; spritz with cooking spray. Cook until a thermometer inserted in chicken reads at least 165°, 15-18 minutes. If desired, serve with ranch dressing, barbecue sauce or mustard.

1 chicken breast half: 353 cal., 18g fat (2g sat. fat), 123mg chol., 230mg sod., 6g carb. (2g sugars, 3g fiber), 41g pro.

TURKEY STUFFED PEPPERS

With this recipe, there's no need to par-cook the peppers first. With an air fryer, you can skip this step and go straight to the stuffing. Ground chicken or beef may be substituted for the turkey.

—Lily Julow, Lawrenceville, GA

PREP: 35 MIN. • COOK: 10 MIN./BATCH • MAKES: 6 SERVINGS

6 medium green or sweet red peppers
1 lb. ground turkey
1 cup ready-to-serve basmati rice
1 cup soft bread crumbs
½ cup frozen peas, thawed
2 green onions, chopped
2 Tbsp. mango chutney
1 Tbsp. canola oil
1½ tsp. Italian seasoning
1 tsp. grated lemon zest
½ tsp. salt
⅓ cup shredded cheddar cheese

1. Cut tops from peppers; remove the seeds. Finely chop tops; discarding stem. In a large skillet, cook turkey over medium heat until no longer pink, 5-7 minutes, breaking into crumbles; drain. Stir in finely chopped pepper tops and cook until crisp-tender, about 2 minutes.

2. Preheat air fryer to 350°. In a large bowl, combine turkey mixture, rice, bread crumbs, peas, green onions, chutney, oil, Italian seasoning, lemon zest and salt. Fill peppers with the turkey mixture.

3. In batches, place peppers on greased tray in air-fryer basket. Cook until peppers are tender, 8-10 minutes. Sprinkle with the cheese. Cook until cheese is melted, 1-2 minutes longer. Serve with additional chutney.

1 stuffed pepper: 269 cal., 11g fat (3g sat. fat), 56mg chol., 392mg sod., 23g carb. (7g sugars, 3g fiber), 19g pro. **Diabetic exchanges:** 2 lean meat, 1 starch, 1 vegetable, 1 fat.

NASHVILLE HOT CHICKEN

I live in Tennessee and love our famous Nashville hot chicken. In an attempt to make it easier to cook, I decided to try it in an air fryer. I'm so glad I did—this is almost better than the original.
—*April Lane, Greeneville, TN*

PREP: 30 MIN. • COOK: 10 MIN./BATCH • MAKES: 6 SERVINGS

2 Tbsp. dill pickle
   juice, divided
2 Tbsp. hot pepper
   sauce, divided
1 tsp. salt, divided
2 lbs. chicken tenderloins
1 cup all-purpose flour
½ tsp. pepper
1 large egg
½ cup buttermilk
   Cooking spray
½ cup olive oil
2 Tbsp. cayenne pepper
2 Tbsp. dark brown sugar
1 tsp. paprika
1 tsp. chili powder
½ tsp. garlic powder
   Dill pickle slices

1. In a bowl or shallow dish, combine 1 Tbsp. pickle juice, 1 Tbsp. hot sauce and ½ tsp. salt. Add chicken tenderloins and turn to coat. Refrigerate, covered, at least 1 hour. Drain, discarding any marinade.

2. Preheat air fryer to 375°. In a shallow bowl, mix the flour, remaining ½ tsp. salt and pepper. In another bowl, whisk egg, buttermilk, remaining 1 Tbsp. pickle juice and 1 Tbsp. hot sauce. Dip chicken in flour to coat both sides; shake off excess. Dip in egg mixture, then again in flour mixture.

3. In batches, arrange chicken in a single layer on well greased tray in air-fryer basket; spritz with cooking spray. Cook until golden brown, 5-6 minutes. Turn; spritz with cooking spray. Cook until golden brown, 5-6 minutes longer.

4. Whisk together the oil, cayenne pepper, brown sugar and seasonings; pour over hot chicken and toss to coat. Serve with dill pickle slices.

5 oz. cooked chicken: 413 cal., 21g fat (3g sat. fat), 96mg chol., 170mg sod., 20g carb. (5g sugars, 1g fiber), 39g pro.

TEST KITCHEN TIP: Nashville Hot Chicken is southern fried chicken seasoned with cayenne pepper for a hot and spicy twist. It's typically served with white bread and sliced pickles. It's a local specialty of Nashville, but the popularity of this dish has spread to other regions of the United States.

SPICY CHICKEN BREASTS

My family adores this chicken recipe. The coating keeps the chicken nice and moist, and with the taste enhanced by marinating, the result is delicious.
—*Stephanie Otten, Byron Center, MI*

PREP: 25 MIN. + MARINATING • COOK: 20 MIN./BATCH • MAKES: 8 SERVINGS

2   cups buttermilk
2   Tbsp. Dijon mustard
2   tsp. salt
2   tsp. hot pepper sauce
1½ tsp. garlic powder
8   bone-in chicken
    breast halves, skin
    removed (8 oz. each)
2   cups soft bread crumbs
1   cup cornmeal
2   Tbsp. canola oil
½   tsp. poultry seasoning
½   tsp. ground mustard
½   tsp. paprika
½   tsp. cayenne pepper
¼   tsp. dried oregano
¼   tsp. dried parsley flakes

1. Preheat air fryer to 375°. In a large bowl, combine the first 5 ingredients. Add chicken and turn to coat. Refrigerate, covered, 1 hour or overnight.

2. Drain chicken, discarding marinade. Combine the remaining ingredients in a shallow dish and stir to combine. Add chicken, 1 piece at a time, and turn to coat. Place in a single layer on greased tray in air-fryer basket. Cook until a thermometer reads 170°, about 20 minutes, turning halfway through cooking. Return all chicken to air fryer; cook to heat through, 2-3 minutes longer.

1 chicken breast half: 352 cal., 9g fat (2g sat. fat), 104mg chol., 562mg sod., 23g carb. (3g sugars, 1g fiber), 41g pro.

FAJITA-STUFFED CHICKEN

I had all the ingredients for fajitas, but instead of heating up my kitchen by using the oven or stovetop, I decided to put my air fryer to work. I have a smaller model, so I wanted to get as much filling as I could in each chicken breast. Cutting slits in the breasts and then filling them made it easy.
—*Joan Hallford, North Richland Hills, TX*

PREP: 20 MIN. • COOK: 15 MIN./BATCH • MAKES: 4 SERVINGS

4 boneless skinless chicken breast halves (6 oz. each)
1 Tbsp. olive oil
1 Tbsp. chili powder
1 tsp. ground cumin
½ tsp. salt
¼ tsp. garlic powder
1 small onion, halved and thinly sliced
½ medium green pepper, thinly sliced
4 oz. cheddar cheese, cut into 4 slices
   Optional: Salsa, sour cream, minced fresh cilantro, jalapeno slices and guacamole

1. Preheat air fryer to 375°. Cut a pocket horizontally in the thickest part of each chicken breast. Fill with onion and green pepper. In a small bowl, combine olive oil and seasonings; rub over chicken.

2. In batches, place chicken on greased tray in air-fryer basket. Cook 6 minutes. Top chicken with cheese slices; secure with toothpicks. Cook until a thermometer inserted in chicken reads at least 165°, 6-8 minutes longer. Discard toothpicks. If desired, serve with toppings of your choice.

1 chicken breast half: 347 cal., 17g fat (7g sat. fat), 126mg chol., 628mg sod., 5g carb. (1g sugars, 1g fiber), 42g pro.

WHY YOU'LL LOVE IT...
"Very easy and delicious! Tasted like traditional chicken fajitas minus the tortilla. The chicken crisped nicely in our air fryer and cooked the chicken very tender and juicy, not overcooked at all. Only recommendation would be to to add the cheese on top during the last few minutes of cooking as not to crisp it too much."
—RUTH, TASTEOFHOME.COM

COCONUT-CRUSTED TURKEY STRIPS

My granddaughter shared these turkey strips with me.
With a plum dipping sauce, they're just the thing for a light supper.
—*Agnes Ward, Stratford, ON*

PREP: 20 MIN. • COOK: 10 MIN./BATCH • MAKES: 6 SERVINGS

2 large egg whites
2 tsp. sesame oil
½ cup sweetened shredded coconut, lightly toasted
½ cup dry bread crumbs
2 Tbsp. sesame seeds, toasted
½ tsp. salt
1½ lbs. turkey breast tenderloins, cut into ½-in. strips
Cooking spray

DIPPING SAUCE
½ cup plum sauce
⅓ cup unsweetened pineapple juice
1½ tsp. prepared mustard
1 tsp. cornstarch

1. Preheat air fryer to 400°. In a shallow bowl, whisk egg whites and oil. In another shallow bowl, mix coconut, bread crumbs, sesame seeds and salt. Dip the turkey in egg mixture, then in coconut mixture, patting to help coating adhere.

2. In batches, place turkey in a single layer on greased tray in air-fryer basket; spritz with cooking spray. Cook until golden brown, 3-4 minutes. Turn; spritz with cooking spray. Cook until golden brown and turkey is no longer pink, 3-4 minutes longer.

3. Meanwhile, in a small saucepan, mix sauce ingredients. Bring to a boil; cook and stir until thickened, 1-2 minutes. Serve with turkey strips.

3 oz. cooked turkey with 2 Tbsp. sauce: 292 cal., 9g fat (3g sat. fat), 45mg chol., 517mg sod., 24g carb. (5g sugars, 1g fiber), 31g pro. **Diabetic exchanges:** 4 lean meat, 1½ starch, ½ fat.

CHAPTER 7

BEEF

It's affordable, versatile and tastes amazing. It's no wonder beef ranks high among cooks from coast to coast. Now you can explore all the ways your air fryer takes this go-to ingredient up a notch. From all-American classics like meat loaf and burgers to special-occasion steaks, bold fajitas and other global-inspired twists, these beefy favorites are sure to please!

SPICED STEAKS WITH CHERRY SAUCE

Who needs to grill? These impressive steaks, topped with a rich cherry sauce, will delight your guests.
—Taste of Home *Test Kitchen*

PREP: 20 MIN. + CHILLING • COOK: 20 MIN. • MAKES: 4 SERVINGS

½ cup dried cherries
¼ cup port wine, warmed
3½ tsp. coarsely ground pepper
1 tsp. brown sugar
¾ tsp. garlic powder
¾ tsp. paprika
¾ tsp. ground coffee
½ tsp. kosher salt
¼ tsp. ground cinnamon
¼ tsp. ground cumin
⅛ tsp. ground mustard
4 beef tenderloin steaks
   (1¼ in. thick and 6 oz. each)
1 Tbsp. butter
1 large shallot, finely chopped
1 cup reduced-sodium
   beef broth
1 tsp. minced fresh thyme
½ cup heavy whipping cream
   Crumbled blue cheese,
   optional

1. In a small bowl, combine cherries and wine; set aside. In a shallow dish, combine pepper, brown sugar, garlic powder, paprika, coffee, salt, cinnamon, cumin and mustard. Add the steaks, 1 at a time, and turn to coat. Cover and refrigerate for 30 minutes.

2. In a small skillet, heat butter over medium-high heat. Add shallot; cook and stir 2 minutes. Add broth and thyme. Bring to a boil; cook until liquid is reduced by half, about 8 minutes. Stir in cream; bring to a boil. Cook until thickened, about 8 minutes, stirring occasionally.

3. Meanwhile, preheat air fryer to 375°. In batches, arrange steaks on greased tray in air-fryer basket. Cook until meat reaches desired doneness (for medium-rare, a thermometer should read 135°; medium, 140°; medium-well, 145°), 3-6 minutes on each side.

4. Stir reserved cherry mixture into cream sauce; serve with steaks. If desired, sprinkle with blue cheese.

1 steak with 3 Tbsp. sauce: 488 cal., 24g fat (13g sat. fat), 117mg chol., 388mg sod., 24g carb. (17g sugars, 1g fiber), 39g pro.

BEEFY SWISS BUNDLES

Kids and adults alike will devour these comforting yet special pockets. With creamy mashed potatoes, gooey cheese and flavorful seasonings, what's not to love?
—Taste of Home *Test Kitchen*

PREP: 20 MIN. • COOK: 10 MIN./BATCH • MAKES: 4 SERVINGS

1   lb. ground beef
1½ cups sliced fresh mushrooms
½   cup chopped onion
1½ tsp. minced garlic
4   tsp. Worcestershire sauce
¾   tsp. dried rosemary, crushed
¾   tsp. paprika
½   tsp. salt
¼   tsp. pepper
1   sheet frozen puff pastry, thawed
⅔   cup refrigerated mashed potatoes
1   cup shredded Swiss cheese
1   large egg
2   Tbsp. water

1. Preheat air fryer to 375°. In a large skillet, cook the beef, mushrooms and onion over medium heat until the meat is no longer pink and vegetables are tender, 8-10 minutes. Add garlic; cook 1 minute longer. Drain. Stir in Worcestershire sauce and seasonings. Remove from the heat; set aside.

2. On a lightly floured surface, roll puff pastry into a 15x13-in. rectangle. Cut into four 7½x6½-in. rectangles. Place about 2 Tbsp. potatoes over each rectangle; spread to within 1 in. of edges. Top each with ¾ cup beef mixture; sprinkle with ¼ cup shredded Swiss cheese.

Freeze option: Freeze unbaked pastries on a parchment-lined baking sheet until firm. Transfer to an airtight container; return to freezer. To use, cook frozen pastries as directed until golden brown and heated through, increasing time to 15-20 minutes.

1 bundle: 706 cal., 42g fat (15g sat. fat), 147mg chol., 809mg sod., 44g carb. (2g sugars, 6g fiber), 35g pro.

STEAK FAJITAS

Zesty salsa and tender strips of steak make these traditional fajitas extra flavorful.
—*Rebecca Baird, Salt Lake City, UT*

TAKES: 30 MIN. • MAKES: 6 SERVINGS

2 large tomatoes, seeded
    and chopped
½ cup diced red onion
¼ cup lime juice
1 jalapeno pepper,
    seeded and minced
3 Tbsp. minced fresh cilantro
2 tsp. ground cumin, divided
¾ tsp. salt, divided
1 beef flank steak
    (about 1½ lbs.)
1 large onion, halved
    and sliced
6 whole wheat tortillas
    (8 in.), warmed
    Optional: Sliced avocado
    and lime wedges

1. For salsa, place first 5 ingredients in a small bowl; stir in 1 tsp. cumin and ¼ tsp. salt. Let stand until serving.

2. Preheat air-fryer to 400°. Sprinkle steak with the remaining cumin and salt. Place on greased tray in air-fryer basket. Cook until the meat reaches desired doneness (for medium-rare, a thermometer should read 135°; medium, 140°; medium-well, 145°), 6-8 minutes per side. Remove from basket and let stand 5 minutes.

3. Meanwhile, place onion on tray in air-fryer basket. Cook until crisp-tender, 2-3 minutes, stirring once. Slice steak thinly across the grain; serve in tortillas with onion and salsa. If desired, serve with avocado and lime wedges.

1 fajita: 309 cal., 9g fat (4g sat. fat), 54mg chol., 498mg sod., 29g carb. (3g sugars, 5g fiber), 27g pro. **Diabetic exchanges:** 4 lean meat, 2 starch.

WHY YOU'LL LOVE IT...
"Love the fresh ingredients and colorful appearance! You can modify the heat by either using all of it in the salsa or by reserving some for those who like things hot. I added some green pepper to this, too, because I like the flavor it adds."
—NH-RESCUE, TASTEOFHOME.COM

PAPAS RELLENAS

A Cuban classic, these crispy-coated potato balls are filled with a savory ground beef mixture known as picadillo. Try them as an appetizer or as part of a meal with a salad and bread. Count on this recipe to satisfy meat-and-potato lovers!
—*Marina Castle Kelley, Canyon Country, CA*

PREP: 45 MIN. • COOK: 15 MIN./BATCH • MAKES: 2½ DOZEN

2½ lbs. potatoes (about
    8 medium), peeled and
    cut into wedges
1 lb. lean ground
    beef (90% lean)
1 small green pepper,
    finely chopped
1 small onion, finely chopped
½ cup tomato sauce
½ cup sliced green olives
    with pimientos
½ cup raisins
1¼ tsp. salt, divided
1¼ tsp. pepper, divided
½ tsp. paprika
1 tsp. garlic powder
2 large eggs, lightly beaten
1 cup seasoned bread crumbs
    Cooking spray

1. Place potatoes in a large saucepan and cover with water. Bring to a boil. Reduce the heat; cover and cook until tender, 15-20 minutes.

2. Meanwhile, in a large skillet, cook beef, green pepper and onion over medium heat until meat is no longer pink; drain. Stir in tomato sauce, olives, raisins, ¼ tsp. salt, ¼ tsp. pepper and paprika; heat through.

3. Drain potatoes; mash with garlic powder and remaining 1 tsp. salt and pepper. Shape 2 Tbsp. potatoes into a patty; place a heaping tablespoon of filling in the center. Shape potatoes around filling, forming a ball. Repeat.

4. Place eggs and bread crumbs in separate shallow bowls. Dip potato balls in eggs, then roll in bread crumbs. Preheat air fryer to 400°. In batches, place in single layer on greased tray in air-fryer basket; spritz with cooking spray. Cook until golden brown, 14-16 minutes.

3 pieces: 625 cal., 46g fat (5g sat. fat), 65mg chol., 642mg sod., 40g carb. (7g sugars, 2g fiber), 13g pro.

STEAK WITH GARLIC BUTTER

This quick and easy entree is definitely restaurant-quality
and sure to become a staple at your house, too!
—Lily Julow, Lawrenceville, GA

TAKES: 20 MIN. • MAKES: 2 SERVINGS

1 beef flat iron steak or
  boneless top sirloin
  steak (¾ lb.)
⅛ tsp. salt
⅛ tsp. pepper
1 Tbsp. butter, softened
1 tsp. minced fresh parsley
½ tsp. minced garlic
¼ tsp. reduced-sodium
  soy sauce

1. Preheat air fryer to 400°. Sprinkle steak with salt and pepper. Place steak on tray in air-fryer basket. Cook until meat reaches desired doneness (for medium-rare, a thermometer should read 135°; medium, 140°; medium-well, 145°), 8-10 minutes, turning halfway through cooking.

2. Meanwhile, combine butter, parsley, garlic and soy sauce. Serve with steak.

4 oz. cooked beef with 2 tsp. garlic butter: 353 cal., 24g fat (11g sat. fat), 125mg chol., 322mg sod., 0 carb. (0 sugars, 0 fiber), 33g pro.

WHY YOU'LL LOVE IT...
"I wanted to add something special to our menu and this simple, flavorful steak was perfect! Easy way to kick an average meal up a notch!"
—SUSEY22, TASTEOFHOME.COM

GROUND BEEF WELLINGTON

Trying new recipes—like this fun twist on Beef Wellington—is one of my favorite hobbies. I replaced the traditional filet mignon with ground beef, while still keeping the beefy goodness.

—Julie Frankamp, Nicollet, MN

PREP: 30 MIN. • COOK: 20 MIN. • MAKES: 2 SERVINGS

½   cup chopped fresh
     mushrooms
1   Tbsp. butter
2   tsp. all-purpose flour
¼   tsp. pepper, divided
½   cup half-and-half cream
1   large egg yolk
2   Tbsp. finely chopped onion
¼   tsp. salt
½   lb. ground beef
1   tube (4 oz.) refrigerated
     crescent rolls
1   large egg, lightly
     beaten, optional
1   tsp. dried parsley flakes

1. Preheat air fryer to 300°. In a saucepan, heat butter over medium-high heat. Add mushrooms; cook and stir until tender, 5-6 minutes. Stir in the flour and ⅛ tsp. pepper until blended. Gradually add cream. Bring to a boil; cook and stir for 2 minutes or until thickened. Remove from the heat and set aside.

2. In a bowl, combine egg yolk, onion, 2 Tbsp. mushroom sauce, salt and remaining ⅛ tsp. pepper. Crumble beef over mixture and mix well. Shape into 2 loaves. Unroll crescent dough and separate into 2 rectangles; press perforations to seal. Place meat loaf on each rectangle. Bring edges together and pinch to seal. If desired, brush with beaten egg.

3. Place Wellingtons in a single layer on greased tray in air-fryer basket. Cook until golden brown and a thermometer inserted into meat loaf reads 160°, 18-22 minutes.

4. Meanwhile, warm remaining sauce over low heat; stir in parsley. Serve sauce with Wellingtons.

1 serving: 585 cal., 38g fat (14g sat. fat), 208mg chol., 865mg sod., 30g carb. (9g sugars, 1g fiber), 29g pro.

STUFFED MEAT LOAF SLICES

These meat loaf swirls are a family favorite often requested for special occasions. We received the recipe from a fellow faculty member when my husband and I were in our first years of teaching.
—*Judy Knaupp, Rickreall, OR*

PREP: 30 MIN. + CHILLING • COOK: 15 MIN./BATCH • MAKES: 6 SERVINGS

2 cups mashed potatoes
  (with added milk and butter)
2 hard-boiled large
  eggs, chopped
½ cup Miracle Whip
⅓ cup grated Parmesan
  cheese
¼ cup chopped celery
1 green onion, chopped
¼ tsp. salt
¼ tsp. ground mustard
¼ tsp. pepper

MEAT LOAF
1 large egg, lightly beaten
¼ cup dry bread crumbs
1 tsp. salt
1¼ lbs. ground beef

SAUCE
½ cup Miracle Whip
¼ cup 2% milk
1 green onion, sliced

1. For filling, mix first 9 ingredients. In a large bowl, combine beaten egg, bread crumbs and salt. Add beef; mix lightly but thoroughly. On a large piece of heavy-duty foil, pat mixture into a 14x8-in. rectangle. Spread filling over top to within 1 in. of edges. Roll up jelly-roll style, starting with a short side, removing foil as you roll. Seal seam and ends; place on a large plate. Refrigerate, covered, overnight.

2. Preheat air fryer to 325°. Cut roll into 6 slices. In batches, place slices on greased tray in air-fryer basket, cut side up. Cook until a thermometer reads at least 160°, 12-15 minutes. Mix the sauce ingredients; serve with meat loaf.

1 slice with 4 tsp. sauce: 439 cal., 28g fat (9g sat. fat), 167mg chol., 1187mg sod., 20g carb. (5g sugars, 1g fiber), 24g pro.

BACON CHEESEBURGERS

This juicy burger only takes minutes to cook in your air fryer.
I top it with crispy bacon, french-fried onions and my special sauce.
—*Elisabeth Larsen, Pleasant Grove, UT*

PREP: 25 MIN. • COOK: 10 MIN. • MAKES: 4 SERVINGS

1 tsp. Worcestershire sauce
1 garlic clove, minced
½ tsp. seasoned salt
¼ tsp. pepper
1 lb. ground beef
4 slices sharp cheddar cheese
¼ cup mayonnaise
2 Tbsp. ketchup
1 Tbsp. cider vinegar
1 Tbsp. honey
4 hamburger buns, split and toasted
8 cooked bacon strips
½ cup french-fried onions
Optional: Lettuce leaves and sliced tomato

1. Preheat air fryer to 350°. In a large bowl, combine the Worcestershire sauce, minced garlic, seasoned salt and pepper. Add ground beef; mix lightly but thoroughly. Shape into four ½-in.-thick patties.

2. In batches, place burgers in a single layer on tray in air-fryer basket. Cook until a thermometer reads 160°, 8-10 minutes, turning halfway through cooking. Remove burgers from basket. Top with cheese; cover until cheese is melted, 1-2 minutes.

3. Meanwhile, in a small bowl, combine mayonnaise, ketchup, vinegar and honey; spread over cut sides of buns. Top the bun bottoms with bacon, burgers, french-fried onions and, if desired, lettuce and tomato. Replace tops.

1 burger: 708 cal., 46g fat (16g sat. fat), 124mg chol., 1277mg sod., 33g carb. (10g sugars, 1g fiber), 39g pro.

KETO MEATBALLS

I lost 130 pounds following a keto diet. This recipe for saucy air-fryer meatballs makes it easy to stay on track. I enjoying them on their own, but they're also delicious over zucchini noodles.
—*Holly Balzer-Harz, Malone, NY*

PREP: 30 MIN. • COOK: 10 MIN. • MAKES: 4 SERVINGS

½ cup grated Parmesan
  cheese
½ cup shredded
  mozzarella cheese
1 large egg, lightly beaten
2 Tbsp. heavy
  whipping cream
1 garlic clove, minced
1 lb. lean ground
  beef (90% lean)

SAUCE
1 can (8 oz.) tomato
  sauce with basil,
  garlic and oregano
2 Tbsp. prepared pesto
¼ cup heavy whipping cream

Preheat air fryer to 350°. In a large bowl, combine the first 5 ingredients. Add beef; mix lightly but thoroughly. Shape into 1½-in. balls. Place in a single layer on greased tray in air-fryer basket; cook until meatballs are lightly browned and cooked through, 8-10 minutes.

Freeze option: Freeze cooled meatballs in freezer containers. To use, partially thaw in refrigerator overnight. Preheat air fryer to 350°. Reheat until heated through, 3-5 minutes. Make sauce as directed.

4 meatballs with ⅓ cup sauce: 404 cal., 27g fat (13g sat. fat), 162mg chol., 799mg sod., 7g carb. (3g sugars, 1g fiber), 31g pro.

TEST KITCHEN TIP: When following a ketogenic diet, participants eat 70% to 75% of their calories as fats, 15% to 20% as protein, and the remaining 5% to 10% as carbohydrates. Protein can include beef, pork, lamb, eggs, fish and chicken. Carbs cannot exceed 30 grams of net carbs (that's carbohydrate grams minus fiber grams), which could include vegetables like cauliflower, kale, bok choy, mushrooms, avocados, peppers and asparagus.

MINI CHIMICHANGAS

My family raves over these Mexican-inspired bites. Infused with green
chiles for extra bite, the beefy snacks are guaranteed to liven up the party!
—*Kathy Rogers, Hudson, OH*

PREP: 1 HOUR • COOK: 10 MIN./BATCH • MAKES: 14 SERVINGS

1   lb. ground beef
1   medium onion, chopped
1   envelope taco seasoning
¾   cup water
3   cups shredded Monterey
    Jack cheese
1   cup sour cream
1   can (4 oz.) chopped
    green chiles, drained
14 egg roll wrappers
1   large egg white,
    lightly beaten
    Cooking spray
    Salsa

1. In a large skillet, cook beef and onion over medium heat until meat is no longer pink; drain. Stir in taco seasoning and water. Bring to a boil. Reduce heat; simmer, uncovered, for 5 minutes, stirring occasionally. Remove from the heat; cool slightly.

2. Preheat air fryer to 375°. In a large bowl, combine cheese, sour cream and chiles. Stir in beef mixture. Place an egg roll wrapper on work surface with 1 point facing you. Place ⅓ cup filling in the center. Fold the bottom one-third of wrapper over filling; fold in the sides.

3. Brush top point with egg white; roll up to seal. Repeat with remaining wrappers and filling. (Keep remaining egg roll wrappers covered with waxed paper to avoid drying out.)

4. In batches, place chimichangas in a single layer on greased tray in air-fryer basket; spritz with cooking spray. Cook until golden brown, 3-4 minutes on each side. Serve warm with salsa and additional sour cream.

1 chimichanga: 294 cal., 15g fat (8g sat. fat), 48mg chol., 618mg sod., 23g carb. (1g sugars, 1g fiber), 16g pro.

CHAPTER 8

SANDWICHES

Savored for lunch or dinner, paired with a steamy cup of soup or even reinvented from last night's leftovers, sandwiches are the ultimate hand-held wonder. Hot, melty, packed with flavor and a cinch to cook in the air fryer, these innovative patties, pockets and other fun twists are your secret to achieving superior sandwichery!

PIGS IN A PONCHO

For pigs in a blanket with a Mexican twist, we add refried beans and green chiles.
Spice it up even more with pepper jack cheese, jalapenos and guacamole.
—*Jennifer Stowell, Deep River, IA*

PREP: 25 MIN. • COOK: 15 MIN./BATCH • MAKES: 8 SERVINGS

8   hot dogs
1   can (16 oz.) refried beans
8   flour tortillas (10 in.)
1   can (4 oz.) chopped
     green chiles
1   can (2¼ oz.) sliced
     ripe olives, drained
2   cups shredded Monterey
     Jack cheese
     Cooking spray
     Optional: Sour cream
     and salsa

1. Preheat air fryer to 375°. Heat hot dogs according to package directions. Spread beans over center of each tortilla; layer with green chiles, olives and cheese. Place hot dog down center of tortilla. Fold bottom and sides of tortilla over filling and roll up.

2. In batches, arrange wraps in a single layer on greased tray in air-fryer basket; spritz with cooking spray. Cook until lightly browned, 6-8 minutes. Turn; spritz with cooking spray. Cook until golden brown and crisp, 6-8 minutes longer. If desired, serve with sour cream and salsa.

1 wrap: 539 cal., 30g fat (14g sat. fat), 50mg chol., 1486mg sod., 46g carb. (4g sugars, 5g fiber), 21g pro.

TEST KITCHEN TIP: To make these pockets a little healthier, try nitrate-free turkey dogs instead of regular beef hot dogs. To help slash fat even more, use fat-free beans and reduce the amount of cheese and sour cream.

PORTOBELLO MELTS

We're always looking for satisfying vegetarian meals, and this one tops the list. These melts are especially delicious in the summer when we have tons of homegrown tomatoes.
—*Amy Smalley, Morehead, KY*

TAKES: 25 MIN. • MAKES: 2 SERVINGS

2 large portobello mushrooms (4 oz. each), stems removed
¼ cup olive oil
2 Tbsp. balsamic vinegar
½ tsp. salt
½ tsp. dried basil
4 tomato slices
2 slices mozzarella cheese
2 slices Italian bread (1 in. thick)
Chopped fresh basil

1. Place mushrooms in a shallow bowl. Mix the oil, vinegar, salt and dried basil; brush onto both sides of mushrooms. Let stand 5 minutes. Reserve remaining marinade. Preheat air fryer to 400°.

2. Place mushrooms on greased tray in air-fryer basket, stem side down. Cook until tender, 3-4 minutes per side. Remove from basket. Top stem sides with tomato and cheese; secure with toothpicks. Cook until cheese is melted, about 1 minute. Remove and keep warm; discard toothpicks.

3. Place bread on tray in air-fryer basket; brush with reserved marinade. Cook until lightly toasted, 2-3 minutes. Top with mushrooms. Sprinkle with chopped basil.

1 open-faced sandwich: 427 cal., 30g fat (4g sat. fat), 4mg chol., 864mg sod., 33g carb. (8g sugars, 4g fiber), 8g pro.

HAM & CHEESE TURNOVERS

I adore the combo of pears, blue cheese and walnuts in a salad, so I turned them into this air-fried turnover recipe—and they were a hit. I added black forest ham to make it a meal in one. Just add a salad of mixed greens with a balsamic vinaigrette and you have a decadent and healthy dinner.

—Trisha Kruse, Eagle, ID

PREP: 20 MIN. • COOK: 10 MIN./BATCH • MAKES: 4 SERVINGS

1 tube (13.8 oz.) refrigerated pizza crust
¼ lb. thinly sliced black forest deli ham
1 medium pear, thinly sliced and divided
¼ cup chopped walnuts, toasted
2 Tbsp. crumbled blue cheese

1. Preheat air fryer to 400°. On a lightly floured surface, unroll pizza crust into a 12-in. square. Cut into 4 squares. Layer ham, half the pear slices, walnuts and blue cheese diagonally over half of each square to within ½ in. of edges. Fold 1 corner over filling to the opposite corner, forming a triangle; press edges with a fork to seal.

2. In batches, arrange turnovers in a single layer on greased tray in air-fryer basket; spritz with cooking spray. Cook until golden brown, 4-6 minutes on each side. Garnish with the remaining pear slices.

1 turnover: 357 cal., 10g fat (2g sat. fat), 16mg chol., 885mg sod., 55g carb. (11g sugars, 3g fiber), 15g pro.

SHRIMP PO'BOYS

Because my husband loves crispy coconut shrimp and po'boys, I combined them with a spicy remoulade for an out-of-this-world sandwich! This air-fryer shrimp goes over big with family and friends and is frequently requested. For catfish po'boys, substitute cornmeal for the coconut and add a few minutes to the cooking time.
—*Marla Clark, Albuquerque, NM*

PREP: 35 MIN. • COOK: 10 MIN./BATCH • MAKES: 4 SERVINGS

½ cup mayonnaise
1 Tbsp. Creole mustard
1 Tbsp. chopped cornichons or dill pickles
1 Tbsp. minced shallot
1½ tsp. lemon juice
⅛ tsp. cayenne pepper

COCONUT SHRIMP

1 cup all-purpose flour
1 tsp. herbes de Provence
½ tsp. sea salt
½ tsp. garlic powder
½ tsp. pepper
¼ tsp. cayenne pepper
1 large egg
½ cup 2% milk
1 tsp. hot pepper sauce
2 cups sweetened shredded coconut
1 lb. uncooked shrimp (26-30 per lb.), peeled and deveined
   Cooking spray
4 hoagie buns, split
2 cups shredded lettuce
1 medium tomato, thinly sliced

1. For remoulade, in a bowl, combine the first 6 ingredients. Refrigerate, covered, until serving.

2. Preheat air fryer to 375°. In a shallow bowl, mix flour, herbes de Provence, sea salt, garlic powder, pepper and cayenne. In a separate shallow bowl, whisk egg, milk and hot pepper sauce. Place coconut in a third shallow bowl. Dip shrimp in flour to coat both sides; shake off excess. Dip in egg mixture, then in coconut, patting to help adhere.

3. In batches, arrange shrimp in a single layer on greased tray in air-fryer basket; spritz with cooking spray. Cook until coconut is lightly browned and shrimp turn pink, 3-4 minutes on each side.

4. Spread cut side of buns with remoulade. Top with shrimp, lettuce and tomato.

1 sandwich: 716 cal., 40g fat (16g sat. fat), 173mg chol., 944mg sod., 60g carb. (23g sugars, 4g fiber), 31g pro.

HERB & CHEESE-STUFFED BURGERS

Tired of the same old ground beef burgers? These quick air-fryer hamburgers, with their creamy cheese filling, will wake up your taste buds.
—*Sherri Cox, Lucasville, OH*

PREP: 20 MIN. • COOK: 15 MIN./BATCH • MAKES: 4 SERVINGS

2 green onions, thinly sliced
2 Tbsp. minced fresh parsley
4 tsp. Dijon mustard, divided
3 Tbsp. dry bread crumbs
2 Tbsp. ketchup
½ tsp. salt
½ tsp. dried rosemary, crushed
¼ tsp. dried sage leaves
1 lb. lean ground beef (90% lean)
2 oz. cheddar cheese, sliced
4 hamburger buns, split
Optional toppings: Lettuce leaves, sliced tomato, mayonnaise and additional ketchup

1. Preheat air fryer to 375°. In a small bowl, combine green onions, parsley and 2 tsp. mustard. In another bowl, mix bread crumbs, ketchup, seasonings and remaining 2 tsp. mustard. Add beef to bread crumb mixture; mix lightly but thoroughly.

2. Shape mixture into 8 thin patties. Place sliced cheese in center of 4 patties; spoon green onion mixture over cheese. Top with remaining patties, pressing edges together firmly, taking care to seal completely.

3. In batches, place burgers in a single layer on tray in air-fryer basket. Cook 8 minutes. Flip; cook until a thermometer inserted in burger reads 160°, 6-8 minutes longer. Serve the burgers on buns, with toppings if desired.

1 burger: 369 cal., 14g fat (6g sat. fat), 79mg chol., 850mg sod., 29g carb. (6g sugars, 1g fiber), 29g pro.

REUBEN CALZONES

I love a Reuben sandwich, so I tried the fillings in a pizza pocket instead of on rye bread. This hand-held dinner is a big-time winner at our house.
—*Nickie Frye, Evansville, IN*

PREP: 15 MIN. • COOK: 10 MIN./BATCH • MAKES: 4 SERVINGS

1 tube (13.8 oz.) refrigerated pizza crust
4 slices Swiss cheese
1 cup sauerkraut, rinsed and well drained
½ lb. sliced cooked corned beef
Thousand Island salad dressing

1. Preheat air fryer to 400°. On a lightly floured surface, unroll pizza crust dough and pat into a 12-in. square. Cut dough into 4 squares. Layer 1 slice cheese and a fourth of the sauerkraut and corned beef diagonally over half of each square to within ½ in. of edges. Fold 1 corner over filling to the opposite corner, forming a triangle; press the edges with a fork to seal. Place 2 calzones in a single layer on greased tray in air-fryer basket.

2. Cook until golden brown, 8-12 minutes, flipping halfway through cooking. Serve with salad dressing.

1 calzone: 430 cal., 17g fat (6g sat. fat), 66mg chol., 1471mg sod., 49g carb. (7g sugars, 2g fiber), 21g pro.

WHY YOU'LL LOVE IT...
"Love this recipe! I used a 15 oz. package of pizza dough instead of the tube of pizza dough and folded the dough up over the top instead of trying to make a triangle. Delish!"
—MWEBBER40, TASTEOFHOME.COM

GREEN TOMATO BLT

I have used this air-frying method on eggplant slices for years and decided to try it on my green tomatoes. It worked! Now my family loves them in BLTs.

—*Jolene Martinelli, Fremont, NH*

PREP: 20 MIN. COOK 10 MIN./BATCH • MAKES: 4 SERVINGS

2 medium green tomatoes (about 10 oz.)
½ tsp. salt
¼ tsp. pepper
1 large egg, beaten
¼ cup all-purpose flour
1 cup panko bread crumbs
 Cooking spray
½ cup reduced-fat mayonnaise
2 green onions, finely chopped
1 tsp. snipped fresh dill or ¼ tsp. dill weed
8 slices whole wheat bread, toasted
8 cooked center-cut bacon strips
4 Bibb or Boston lettuce leaves

1. Preheat air fryer to 350°. Cut each tomato crosswise into 4 slices. Sprinkle with salt and pepper. Place egg, flour and bread crumbs in separate shallow bowls. Dip tomato slices in flour, shaking off excess, then dip into egg, and finally into bread crumb mixture, patting to help adhere.

2. In batches, arrange tomato slices in a single layer on greased tray in the air-fryer basket; spritz with cooking spray. Cook until golden brown, 4-6 minutes. Turn; spritz with cooking spray. Cook until golden brown, 4-6 minutes longer.

3. Meanwhile, mix the mayonnaise, green onions and dill. Layer each of 4 slices of bread with 2 bacon strips, 1 lettuce leaf and 2 tomato slices. Spread mayonnaise mixture over remaining slices of bread; place over top. Serve immediately.

1 sandwich: 390 cal., 17g fat (3g sat. fat), 45mg chol., 1006mg sod., 45g carb. (7g sugars, 5g fiber), 16g pro.

CHICKPEA & RED ONION BURGERS

When chilly days arrive and we retire the grill to the garage, I bake a batch of air-fryer chickpea burgers. Even die-hard meat eaters can't resist them.
—*Lily Julow, Lawrenceville, GA*

TAKES: 30 MIN. • MAKES: 6 SERVINGS

1 large red onion, thinly sliced
¼ cup fat-free red wine vinaigrette
2 cans (15 oz. each) chickpeas or garbanzo beans, rinsed and drained
⅓ cup chopped walnuts
¼ cup toasted wheat germ or dry bread crumbs
¼ cup packed fresh parsley sprigs
2 large eggs
1 tsp. curry powder
½ tsp. pepper
Cooking spray
⅓ cup fat-free mayonnaise
2 tsp. Dijon mustard
6 sesame seed hamburger buns, split and toasted
6 lettuce leaves
3 Tbsp. thinly sliced fresh basil leaves

1. Preheat air fryer to 375°. In a small bowl, mix the onion and vinaigrette. Place chickpeas, walnuts, wheat germ and parsley in a food processor; pulse until blended. Add eggs, curry and pepper; process until smooth.

2. Shape into 6 patties. In batches, place the patties in a single layer on greased tray in air-fryer basket, spray with cooking spray. Cook until a thermometer reads 160°, 8-10 minutes, flipping halfway through.

3. In a small bowl, mix mayonnaise and mustard; spread over cut sides of buns. Serve patties on buns with lettuce, basil and onion mixture.

1 burger: 381 cal., 13g fat (2g sat. fat), 62mg chol., 697mg sod., 54g carb. (10g sugars, 9g fiber), 16g pro.

TACO TWISTS

Skip ordinary flour or corn tortillas for your tacos. For a mouthwatering change of pace, bake the seasoned beef in flaky, golden crescent rolls in your air fryer. My family enjoys these for a warm lunch or light dinner.

—*Carla Kreider, Quarryville, PA*

PREP: 15 MIN. • COOK: 20 MIN. • MAKES: 4 SERVINGS

⅓ lb. ground beef
1 large onion, chopped
⅔ cup shredded cheddar cheese
⅓ cup salsa
3 Tbsp. canned chopped green chiles
¼ tsp. garlic powder
¼ tsp. hot pepper sauce
⅛ tsp. salt
⅛ tsp. ground cumin
1 tube (8 oz.) refrigerated crescent rolls
Optional: Shredded lettuce, sliced ripe olives, chopped tomatoes, sliced seeded jalapeno pepper

1. Preheat air fryer to 300°. In a large skillet, cook beef and onion over medium heat until meat is no longer pink; drain. Stir in the cheese, salsa, chiles, garlic powder, hot pepper sauce, salt and cumin. Unroll crescent roll dough and separate into 4 rectangles; press perforations to seal. Place ½ cup meat mixture in center of each rectangle. Bring 4 corners to the center and twist; pinch to seal.

2. In batches, place in a single layer on greased tray in air-fryer basket. Cook until golden brown, 18-22 minutes. If desired, serve with toppings of your choice.

1 taco twist: 371 cal., 21g fat (5g sat. fat), 42mg chol., 752mg sod., 30g carb. (8g sugars, 1g fiber), 16g pro.

TUNA PATTIES

My family was so accustomed to a typical beef burger that they were hesitant to try these when I first made them. Any skepticism disappeared after one bite.
—*Kim Stoller, Smithville, OH*

TAKES: 30 MIN. • MAKES: 4 SERVINGS

1   large egg, lightly beaten
½   cup dry bread crumbs
½   cup finely chopped celery
⅓   cup mayonnaise
¼   cup finely chopped onion
2   Tbsp. chili sauce
1   pouch (6.4 oz.) light
    tuna in water
4   hamburger buns,
    split and toasted
    Optional: Lettuce leaves
    and sliced tomato

1. Preheat air fryer to 350°. In a small bowl, combine first 6 ingredients; fold in tuna. Shape into 4 patties.

2. In batches, place the patties in a single layer on greased tray in air-fryer basket. Cook until lightly browned, 5-6 minutes per side. Serve on buns. If desired, top with lettuce and tomato.

1 burger: 366 cal., 17g fat (3g sat. fat), 64mg chol., 665mg sod., 35gcarb. (6g sugars, 2g fiber), 17g pro.

WHY YOU'LL LOVE IT...
"Easy, delicious meal! I used fat-free Miracle Whip instead of mayo and placed the patties in pita bread instead of buns. Awesome! I also put cucumber slices on the burger to give it a nice crunch. My husband loved this meal. He's already asked me to make it again!"
—MEDSTUDENTWIFE, TASTEOFHOME.COM

CHAPTER 9

SWEETS & DESSERTS

Now that you've mastered making dinner in your air fryer, it's time for dessert! From crisp and crunchy cookies to molten lava cakes, these air-fried desserts prove this ingenious kitchen invention is the new go-to appliance for the best sweet treats!

CHOCOLATE CHIP OATMEAL COOKIES

I am crazy about chocolate chips, and this chewy cookie has enough to satisfy me. My husband nibbles on the dough, and my kids love the cookies. This big batch is perfect, even for our small family.
—Diane Neth, Menno, SD

PREP: 20 MIN. • COOK: 10 MIN./BATCH • MAKES: 6 DOZEN

1 cup butter, softened
¾ cup sugar
¾ cup packed brown sugar
2 large eggs, room temperature
1 tsp. vanilla extract
3 cups quick-cooking oats
1½ cups all-purpose flour
1 pkg. (3.4 oz.) instant vanilla pudding mix
1 tsp. baking soda
1 tsp. salt
2 cups (12 oz.) semisweet chocolate chips
1 cup chopped nuts

1. Preheat air fryer to 325°. In a large bowl, cream butter and sugars until light and fluffy, 5-7 minutes. Beat in eggs and vanilla. In another bowl, whisk oats, flour, dry pudding mix, baking soda and salt; gradually beat into creamed mixture. Stir in chocolate chips and nuts.

2. Drop dough by tablespoonfuls onto baking sheets; flatten slightly. In batches, place 1 in. apart on greased tray in air-fryer basket. Cook until lightly browned, 8-10 minutes. Remove to wire racks to cool.

1 cookie: 102 cal., 5g fat (3g sat. fat), 12mg chol., 82mg sod., 13g carb. (8g sugars, 1g fiber), 2g pro.

WHY YOU'LL LOVE IT...
"These cookies were amazing! Chewy and delicious. Only took 6-8 minutes in our air fryer. We will absolutely make these again."
—BECKY, TASTEOFHOME.COM

S'MORES CRESCENT ROLLS

Here's how to score indoor s'mores: Grab crescent dough and Nutella.
Then invite the kids to help with this rolled-up version of the campfire classic.
—*Cathy Trochelman, Brookfield, WI*

PREP: 15 MIN. • COOK: 10 MIN./BATCH • MAKES: 8 SERVINGS

1 tube (8 oz.) refrigerated
   crescent rolls
¼ cup Nutella, divided
2 whole graham
   crackers, broken up
2 Tbsp. milk chocolate chips
⅔ cup miniature
   marshmallows

1. Preheat air fryer to 300°. Unroll crescent dough; separate into 8 triangles. Place 1 tsp. Nutella at the wide end of each triangle. Sprinkle each with graham cracker pieces, chocolate chips and marshmallows; roll up.

2. In batches, arrange rolls, point side down, in a single layer on greased tray in air-fryer basket. Curve to form crescents. Cook until golden brown, 8-10 minutes. In a microwave, warm the remaining Nutella to reach a drizzling consistency; spoon over rolls. Serve warm.

1 roll: 191 cal., 9g fat (1g sat. fat), 1mg chol., 245mg sod., 26g carb. (13g sugars, 1g fiber), 3g pro.

CHOCOLATE BREAD PUDDING

Here's a rich, comforting dessert that's easy to make in the air fryer. It's a fun recipe because the chocolate sets it apart from traditional bread pudding.
—*Mildred Sherrer, Fort Worth, TX*

PREP: 15 MIN. + STANDING • COOK: 15 MIN. • MAKES: 2 SERVINGS

2   oz. semisweet chocolate, chopped
½   cup half-and-half cream
⅔   cup sugar
½   cup 2% milk
1   large egg, room temperature
1   tsp. vanilla extract
¼   tsp. salt
4   slices day-old bread, crusts removed and cut into cubes (about 3 cups)
    Optional toppings: Confectioners' sugar and whipped cream

1. In a small microwave-safe bowl, melt chocolate; stir until smooth. Stir in cream; set aside.

2. In a large bowl, whisk sugar, milk, egg, vanilla and salt. Stir in chocolate mixture. Add bread cubes and toss to coat. Let stand 15 minutes.

3. Preheat air fryer to 325°. Spoon bread mixture into 2 greased 8-oz. ramekins. Place on tray in air-fryer basket. Cook until a knife inserted in the center comes out clean, 12-15 minutes.

4. If desired, top with confectioners' sugar and whipped cream.

1 serving: 729 cal., 22g fat (12g sat. fat), 128mg chol., 674mg sod., 107g carb. (81g sugars, 2g fiber), 14g pro.

TEST KITCHEN TIP: Most leftover breads work well in this recipe—if it'll make good French toast, it'll make good bread pudding. In general, soft and airy breads work best.

LEMON SLICE SUGAR COOKIES

Here's a refreshing variation of my grandmother's classic sugar cookie recipe.
Lemon pudding mix and icing add a subtle tartness that tingles your taste buds.
—Melissa Turkington, Camano Island, WA

PREP: 15 MIN. + CHILLING • COOK: 10 MIN./ BATCH + COOLING • MAKES: ABOUT 2 DOZEN

½ cup unsalted butter,
  softened
1 pkg. (3.4 oz.) instant
  lemon pudding mix
½ cup sugar
1 large egg, room
  temperature
2 Tbsp. 2% milk
1½ cups all-purpose flour
1 tsp. baking powder
¼ tsp. salt

ICING

⅔ cup confectioners' sugar
2 to 4 tsp. lemon juice

1. In a large bowl, cream butter, pudding mix and sugar until light and fluffy, 5-7 minutes. Beat in egg and milk. In another bowl, whisk flour, baking powder and salt; gradually beat into creamed mixture.

2. Divide dough in half. On a lightly floured surface, shape each into a 6-in.-long roll. Wrap and refrigerate 3 hours or until firm.

3. Preheat air fryer to 325°. Unwrap and cut dough crosswise into ½-in. slices. In batches, place slices in a single layer on greased tray in air-fryer basket. Cook until the edges are light brown, 8-12 minutes. Cool in basket 2 minutes. Remove to wire racks to cool completely.

4. In a small bowl, mix confectioners' sugar and enough lemon juice to reach a drizzling consistency. Drizzle over cookies. Let stand until set.

To make ahead: Dough can be made 2 days in advance. Wrap and place in a resealable container. Store in the refrigerator.

Freeze option: Place wrapped logs in a resealable container and freeze. To use, unwrap frozen logs and cut into slices. Cook as directed, increasing time by 1-2 minutes.

1 cookie: 110 cal., 4g fat (2g sat. fat), 18mg chol., 99mg sod., 17g carb. (11g sugars, 0 fiber), 1g pro.

HONEY CINNAMON ROLL-UPS

These cinnamony treats remind me of baklava, but with only a few easy ingredients, it's a fraction of the work. My Aunt Adele shared the recipe with me, and I think of her whenever I make it.
—*Sue Falk, Sterling Heights, MI*

PREP: 35 MIN. + COOLING • COOK: 10 MIN./BATCH • MAKES: 24 SERVINGS

- 2 cups ground walnuts, toasted
- ¼ cup sugar
- 2 tsp. ground cinnamon
- 12 sheets frozen phyllo dough, thawed
- ½ cup butter, melted

SYRUP
- ½ cup honey
- ½ cup sugar
- ½ cup water
- 1 Tbsp. lemon juice

1. Preheat air fryer to 325°. Combine walnuts, sugar and cinnamon.

2. Place 1 sheet of phyllo dough on a 15x12-in. piece of waxed paper; brush with butter. Place a second phyllo sheet on top, brushing it with butter. (Keep remaining phyllo covered with a damp towel to prevent it from drying out.) Sprinkle with ¼ cup walnut mixture. Using waxed paper, roll up tightly jelly-roll style, starting with a long side, removing paper as you roll. Slice roll into 4 smaller rolls. Brush with butter; secure with toothpicks. Repeat with remaining phyllo dough and ¼ cups of walnut mixture. In batches, place in a single layer on greased tray in air-fryer basket. Cook until light brown, 9-11 minutes. Cool on a wire rack. Discard toothpicks.

3. Meanwhile, in a small saucepan, combine syrup ingredients. Bring to a boil. Reduce heat; simmer 5 minutes. Cool 10 minutes. Transfer cinnamon rolls to a serving platter; drizzle with syrup. Sprinkle with remaining walnut mixture.

1 cinnamon rollup: 140 cal., 8g fat (3g sat. fat), 10mg chol., 56mg sod., 17g carb. (13g sugars, 1g fiber), 2g pro.

CARIBBEAN WONTONS

I first served these fresh and fruity treats as an appetizer at a summer luau. My family and friends now enjoy them as a dessert for special occasions throughout the year.
—*Melissa Pelkey Hass, Waleska, GA*

PREP: 30 MIN. • COOK: 10 MIN./BATCH • MAKES: 2 DOZEN (1¼ CUPS SAUCE)

4 oz. cream cheese, softened
¼ cup sweetened shredded coconut
¼ cup mashed ripe banana
2 Tbsp. chopped walnuts
2 Tbsp. canned crushed pineapple
1 cup marshmallow creme
24 wonton wrappers
Cooking spray

SAUCE
1 lb. fresh strawberries, hulled
¼ cup sugar
1 tsp. cornstarch
Confectioners' sugar and ground cinnamon

1. Preheat air fryer to 350°. In a small bowl, beat cream cheese until smooth. Stir in coconut, banana, walnuts and pineapple. Fold in marshmallow creme.

2. Position a wonton wrapper with 1 point toward you. Keep remaining wrappers covered with a damp paper towel until ready to use. Place 2 tsp. filling in the center of wrapper. Moisten edges with water; fold opposite corners together over filling and press to seal. Repeat with remaining wrappers and filling.

3. In batches, arrange wontons in a single layer on greased tray in air-fryer basket; spritz with cooking spray. Cook until golden brown and crisp, 10-12 minutes.

4. Meanwhile, place strawberries in a food processor; cover and process until pureed. In a small saucepan, combine sugar and cornstarch. Stir in pureed strawberries. Bring to a boil; cook and stir until thickened, about 2 minutes. If desired, strain the berry mixture, reserving sauce; discard seeds. Sprinkle wontons with confectioners' sugar and cinnamon. Serve with sauce.

1 wonton with 1½ tsp. sauce: 83 cal., 3g fat (1g sat. fat), 5mg chol., 67mg sod., 13g carb. (7g sugars, 1g fiber), 1g pro.

PEPPERMINT LAVA CAKES

It never ceases to amaze to see warm chocolate pudding ooze out of the center of this tender chocolate cake. These cakes are a showstopper on a plate! Serve lava cakes with whipped cream or ice cream.
—*Carolyn Crotser, Colorado Springs, CO*

TAKES: 30 MIN. • MAKES: 4 SERVINGS

⅔ cup semisweet
   chocolate chips
½ cup butter, cubed
1 cup confectioners' sugar
2 large eggs,
   room temperature
2 large egg yolks,
   room temperature
1 tsp. peppermint extract
6 Tbsp. all-purpose flour
2 Tbsp. finely crushed
   peppermint candies,
   optional

1. Preheat air fryer to 375°. In a microwave-safe bowl, melt chocolate chips and butter for 30 seconds; stir until smooth. Whisk in confectioners' sugar, eggs, egg yolks and extract until blended. Fold in flour.

2. Generously grease and flour four 4-oz. ramekins; pour batter into ramekins. Do not overfill. Place ramekins on tray in air-fryer basket; cook until a thermometer reads 160° and edges of cakes are set, 10-12 minutes. Do not overcook.

3. Remove from basket; let stand 5 minutes. Carefully run a knife around sides of ramekins several times to loosen cake; invert onto dessert plates. Sprinkle with crushed candies. Serve immediately.

1 serving: 563 cal., 36g fat (21g sat. fat), 246mg chol., 226mg sod., 57g carb. (45g sugars, 2g fiber), 7g pro.

TEST KITCHEN TIP: Peppermint typically only makes a prominent appearance in grocery aisles during the holidays (bring on the peppermint bark, candy canes and peppermint patties!), but the refreshing flavor is perfect to enjoy year-round. Its strong flavor is best-suited for sweet dishes, especially those with chocolate, which is why your fondest memories of peppermint are probably when it's crushed on top of a ooey-gooey lava cake like this one or swirled into a steamy mug of hot cocoa.

HONEYED PEARS IN PUFF PASTRY

A honey of a salute to late-summer pear season, this cozy dessert looks both elegant and decadent. Wrapped in puff pastry, the pears resemble little beehives.

—*Heather Baird, Knoxville, TN*

PREP: 25 MIN. • COOK: 15 MIN. • MAKES: 4 SERVINGS

4 small pears
4 cups water
2 cups sugar
1 cup honey
1 small lemon, halved
3 cinnamon sticks (3 in.)
6 to 8 whole cloves
1 vanilla bean
1 sheet frozen puff pastry, thawed
1 large egg, lightly beaten

1. Core pears from bottom, leaving stems intact. Peel pears; cut ¼ in. from the bottom of each to level if necessary.

2. In a large saucepan, combine water, sugar, honey, lemon halves, cinnamon and cloves. Split vanilla bean and scrape seeds; add bean and seeds to sugar mixture. Bring to a boil. Reduce heat; place pears on their sides in saucepan and poach, uncovered, until almost tender, basting occasionally with the poaching liquid, 16-20 minutes.

3. Remove pears with a slotted spoon; cool slightly. Strain and reserve 1½ cups poaching liquid; set aside.

4. Preheat air fryer to 325°. Unfold puff pastry on a lightly floured surface. Cut into ½-in.-wide strips. Brush lightly with beaten egg. Starting at the bottom of a pear, wrap a pastry strip around pear, adding additional strips until pear is completely wrapped in pastry. Repeat with remaining pears and puff pastry.

5. Place the pears in a single layer on greased tray in air-fryer basket. Cook until golden brown, 12-15 minutes.

6. Meanwhile, bring reserved poaching liquid to a boil; cook until liquid is thick and syrupy, about 10 minutes. Place pears on dessert plates and drizzle with syrup. Serve warm.

1 pear with 3 Tbsp. syrup: 536 cal., 18g fat (4g sat. fat), 47mg chol., 223mg sod., 92g carb. (50g sugars, 9g fiber), 7g pro.

APPLE PIE EGG ROLLS

These easy apple pie egg rolls can be prepared as needed, using egg roll wrappers as a vessel for the fruit instead of traditional pie crust. The air-fryer method results in a crispy, crunchy crust with a tender, juicy filling. Flavored cream cheese spread may be used instead of plain, if desired.

—*Sheila Joan Suhan, Scottdale, PA*

PREP: 25 MIN. • COOK: 15 MIN./BATCH • MAKES: 8 SERVINGS

3 cups chopped peeled tart apples
½ cup packed light brown sugar
2½ tsp. ground cinnamon, divided
1 tsp. cornstarch
8 egg roll wrappers
½ cup spreadable cream cheese
 Butter-flavored cooking spray
1 Tbsp. sugar
⅔ cup hot caramel ice cream topping

1. Preheat air fryer to 400°. In a small bowl, combine apples, brown sugar, 2 tsp. cinnamon and cornstarch. With a corner of an egg roll wrapper facing you, spread 1 scant Tbsp. cream cheese to within 1 in. of edges. Place ⅓ cup apple mixture just below center of wrapper. (Cover remaining wrappers with a damp paper towel until ready to use.)

2. Fold bottom corner over filling; moisten remaining wrapper edges with water. Fold side corners toward center over filling. Roll egg roll up tightly, pressing at tip to seal. Repeat.

3. In batches, arrange egg rolls in a single layer on greased tray in air-fryer basket; spritz with cooking spray. Cook until golden brown, 5-6 minutes. Turn; spritz with cooking spray. Cook until golden brown and crisp, 5-6 minutes longer. Combine sugar and remaining ½ tsp. cinnamon; roll hot egg rolls in mixture. Serve with caramel sauce.

1 roll: 273 cal., 4g fat (2g sat. fat), 13mg chol., 343mg sod., 56g carb. (35g sugars, 2g fiber), 5g pro.

LIME & GIN COCONUT MACAROONS

I took these lime and coconut macaroons to our annual cookie exchange, where we name a queen. I won the crown!
—*Milissa Kirkpatrick, Palestine, TX*

PREP: 20 MIN. • BAKE: 5 MIN./BATCH • MAKES: ABOUT 2½ DOZEN

4 large egg whites, room temperature
⅔ cup sugar
3 Tbsp. gin
1½ tsp. grated lime zest
¼ tsp. salt
¼ tsp. almond extract
1 pkg. (14 oz.) sweetened shredded coconut
½ cup all-purpose flour
8 oz. white baking chocolate, melted

1. Preheat air fryer to 350°. Whisk the first 6 ingredients until blended. In another bowl, toss coconut with flour; stir in egg white mixture.

2. In batches, place by tablespoonfuls 1 in. apart on greased tray in air-fryer basket. Cook until browned, 4-5 minutes. Remove to wire racks to cool.

3. Dip bottoms of macaroons into melted chocolate, allowing excess to drip off. Place on waxed paper; let stand until set. Store in an airtight container.

1 cookie: 133 cal., 7g fat (6g sat. fat), 0 chol., 67mg sod., 17g carb. (15g sugars, 1g fiber), 2g pro.

TEST KITCHEN TIP: You can also dip these macaroons in melted milk or dark chocolate.

SCOTTISH SHORTBREAD

This was my mother's recipe, and she passed it on to me. I make a triple batch
of it each year at Christmas, to enjoy and to give as gifts.
—*Rose Mabee, Selkirk, MB*

PREP: 15 MIN. • COOK: 10 MIN./BATCH + COOLING • MAKES: 4 DOZEN

2 cups butter, softened
1 cup packed brown sugar
4 to 4½ cups all-purpose flour

1. Preheat air fryer to 290°. Cream butter and brown sugar until light and fluffy. Add 3¾ cups flour; mix well. Turn dough onto a floured surface; knead for 5 minutes, adding enough remaining flour to form a soft dough.

2. Roll to ½-in. thickness. Cut into 3x1-in. strips; prick with a fork. Place 1 in. apart on ungreased tray in air-fryer basket. Cook until cookies are set and lightly browned, 7-9 minutes. Cool in basket 2 minutes; remove to wire racks to cool completely.

1 cookie: 123 cal., 8g fat (5g sat. fat), 20mg chol., 62mg sod., 12g carb. (5g sugars, 0 fiber), 1g pro.

WHY YOU'LL LOVE IT...
"I love shortbread and the fact that it is so simple to make. I added about a teaspoon of vanilla because I think it is a great addition. You can also drizzle chocolate on top to dress it up a bit more."
—HCHAMBERS, TASTEOFHOME.COM

EQUIVALENT MEASURES

3 teaspoons = 1 tablespoon	**16 tablespoons** = 1 cup
4 tablespoons = ¼ cup	**2 cups** = 1 pint
5⅓ tablespoons = ⅓ cup	**4 cups** = 1 quart
8 tablespoons = ½ cup	**4 quarts** = 1 gallon

FOOD EQUIVALENTS

Macaroni	1 cup (3½ ounces) uncooked = 2½ cups cooked
Noodles, Medium	3 cups (4 ounces) uncooked = 4 cups cooked
Popcorn	⅓ - ½ cup unpopped = 8 cups popped
Rice, Long Grain	1 cup uncooked = 3 cups cooked
Rice, Quick-Cooking	1 cup uncooked = 2 cups cooked
Spaghetti	8 ounces uncooked = 4 cups cooked
Bread	1 slice = ¾ cup soft crumbs, ¼ cup fine dry crumbs
Graham Crackers	7 squares = ½ cup finely crushed
Buttery Round Crackers	12 crackers = ½ cup finely crushed
Saltine Crackers	14 crackers = ½ cup finely crushed
Bananas	1 medium = ⅓ cup mashed
Lemons	1 medium = 3 tablespoons juice, 2 teaspoons grated peel
Limes	1 medium = 2 tablespoons juice, 1½ teaspoons grated peel
Oranges	1 medium = ¼ -⅓ cup juice, 4 teaspoons grated peel

Cabbage	1 head = 5 cups shredded	**Green Pepper**	1 large = 1 cup chopped
Carrots	1 pound = 3 cups shredded	**Mushrooms**	½ pound = 3 cups sliced
Celery	1 rib = ½ cup chopped	**Onions**	1 medium = ½ cup chopped
Corn	1 ear fresh = ⅔ cup kernels	**Potatoes**	3 medium = 2 cups cubed
Almonds	1 pound = 3 cups chopped	**Pecan Halves**	1 pound = 4½ cups chopped
Ground Nuts	3¾ ounces = 1 cup	**Walnuts**	1 pound = 3¾ cups chopped

EASY SUBSTITUTIONS

WHEN YOU NEED...		USE...
Baking Powder	1 teaspoon	½ teaspoon cream of tartar + ¼ teaspoon baking soda
Buttermilk	1 cup	1 tablespoon lemon juice or vinegar + enough milk to measure 1 cup (let stand 5 minutes before using)
Cornstarch	1 tablespoon	2 tablespoons all-purpose flour
Honey	1 cup	1¼ cups sugar + ¼ cup water
Half-and-Half Cream	1 cup	1 tablespoon melted butter + enough whole milk to measure 1 cup
Onion	1 small, chopped (⅓ cup)	1 teaspoon onion powder or 1 tablespoon dried minced onion
Tomato Juice	1 cup	½ cup tomato sauce + ½ cup water
Tomato Sauce	2 cups	¾ cup tomato paste + 1 cup water
Unsweetened Chocolate	1 square (1 ounce)	3 tablespoons baking cocoa + 1 tablespoon shortening or oil
Whole Milk	1 cup	½ cup evaporated milk + ½ cup water